4-4-2

- Characteristics
- Schemes
- Coaching
- Exercises

REEDSWAIN PUBLISHING

**Library of Congress
Cataloging - in - Publication Data**

4-4-2
Massimo Lucchesi, Mauro Viviani,
Marco Ceccomori, Andrea Riva
Luca Prestigiacomo

ISBN No. 1-59164-065-2
Lib. of Congress Catalog No. 2003109587
© 2003

Editing
Bryan R. Beaver

Printed by
DATA REPRODUCTIONS
Auburn, Michigan

Reedswain Publishing
612 Pughtown Road
Spring City, PA 19475
800.331.5191
www.reedswain.com
info@reedswain.com

CONTENTS

INTRODUCTION

What if we could have more than one chef in attendance in a restaurant; just imagine if, in collaboration with the head waiter, each of them could prepare his best dish for us from the starter to the dessert ...

It is quite an unusual idea to tell the truth, and yet that was our basic starting point. Going on from there to exploit the potential of the internet and our virtual market square, www.allenatore.net, we have now managed to complete a project that is probably unique (as a conception at least) in the Italian literary panorama dedicated to football. Books are normally either written by a single individual (at most by two) or they are collections of separate contributions not strictly connected in origin. The text you are about to read was not composed by a single author, but has drawn on individual contributions given in by various people working in a team under my coordination. Of course, each single member of the team had a specific task or outline, which he was expected to develop in his own way; but, as the separate contributions reached their final stages, they then 'did the rounds' of the group as a whole so that they could be further enriched by each member's experience and ideas.

All this was carried out in order to enhance the final all round quality of the work. We hope that the text will now become a means of learning and comparison for everyone, in exactly the same way that writing it has been for those of us who were involved all this time in the accomplishment of the project. As we have already said, the whole plan was made easier by the use of the internet, which was responsible in the first place for allowing me to contact and get to know the members of the team, and which, more generally, helps us today to cut down barriers and even prejudices with just a little click.

I am truly proud of the work we have carried out. It is, I feel, more important than ever today to compare your ideas and to interact between as many people as possible so as to broaden the single individual's point of view and to open out new horizons and new ideas.

Here then is my personal introduction to the various authors with whom I have shared this positive and fascinating experience:

MARCO CECCOMORI: Marco was born in Pietrasanta, in Versilia, July 13 1972. He has a degree in Political Science and has always been a football fan. A problem with his knee forced him to hang up his football boots, and, just a little later, to put on the clothes of the coach. At present he is training the Allievi B of one of the best known and admired soccer clubs for young players in Tuscany (Margine Coperta, Atalanta's Youth Center in the Tuscan Region). He began working as a coach, however, in nearby Marina di Pietrasanta, where, for some 6 years, he trained all age groups of the Youth Sector - achieving excellent results. Serious, meticulous and scrupulously well-prepared, Marco is always on the look out for ways of extending his competence. His principle contribution here was an examination of how to teach the defense phase.

LUCA PRESTIGIACOMO: Born on June 7 1982, Luca is by far the youngest of the group. But, if his youth is the first surprise, what really struck me about him is the way he can grasp and analyze a soccer match in its totality even though he has never actually coached. Since 1991 he has been 'using' the Meazza Stadium in Milan (where AC Milan are at home) to study the various moves and countermoves carried out by the coaches there - and to make them his own! With the passing of time he has had the opportunity to refine his personal studies going to watch the training sessions of other professional teams. Sacchi and Zeman are the two coaches who have - on account of the spectacular nature and the philosophy of play put into act by their teams - passed on to him this passion for the in-depth study of the tactical aspects of the game. At present Luca is studying Science of Communication at the Catholic University of Milan, and he is following with particular attention the progress of the coach Luigi Del Neri, whose success he had already foreseen in the past. His most important contribution here was to the part of the book that considers the face off between the 4-4-2 and other systems.

ANDREA RIVA: Andrea was born in Lecco, on February 5 1974. After finishing the Scientific High School in his home town with full marks, he enrolled in the Faculty of Physics in the State University of Milan, from which he is soon to graduate. At an early age, he, too, began to take a particular interest in teaching soccer - particularly those aspects related tactics and techniques. His passion for soccer has led him to teach himself as much as he could about the sport by following training sessions in every category and level. He is the 'player' of the group, because for the last 15 years you will have found him - between one injury and another - on the playing fields in the suburbs of Lecco. For us, Andrea developed themes connected with teaching the attacking phase.

MAURO VIVIANI: Born in Leghorn, July 3 1949, of the four members of the group, Mauro is the one with the most experience. Down the years, his career as professional coach has seen him sitting on the bench in the Pisa of the Anconetani years, and in Perugia. Apart from his direct experience, the two things about Mauro that have struck me most in these months of collaboration have been his passion for soccer and his enthusiasm. It was Mauro's task to develop the part of the book which would probably be the most rigid and inflexible, but his contribution in describing the various characteristics of the system and the players was absolutely fundamental.

MASSIMO LUCCHESI: my role in the group was only that of coordinator. Just as no coach could get good results with bad players, so I am sure no coordinator could complete a work of quality without a team of distinction. I wish, therefore, to thank all four authors who have 'played' this particular match and who have given concrete form to what was initially only an idea.

It goes without saying that, like anyone who wants to learn and improve, we are always open to discussion: All you need to do is click: www.allenatore.net.

CHAPTER 1

THE 4-4-2 IN ACTION: INSTRUCTIONS AND THE CHOICE OF PLAYERS

Mauro Viviani

THE COACH:
CAUGHT BETWEEN FICTION AND REALITY

For a coach the best period in the whole soccer season is surely when, after having worked out an agreement concerning programs and monetary retribution, he can get down to work in his new club. For the moment the managers are doing everything they can to follow and execute his indications, the press are warming to him, and even the fans credit him with respect and affection, foreseeing that he will be the new 'unbeatable leader' of their forces. After the initial friendlies and the first Cup matches - if they have not gone as well as was hoped - the inevitable doubts will start jumping out at you, the first misunderstandings, the first more or less aggressive skepticism on the part of the management, the press, the fans.
From that moment on, the bench on which the coach must continue to sit will just get hotter and hotter, each match will soon turn into a last ditch affair, and his work, continually under scrutiny by some microscope or other, have one way, and one way only, to turn the tide - VICTORY. Otherwise ... a slap on the back at best, 'still friends, eh?' - and before you know it, another has taken your place and the round begins again. This is soccer ... or so they say. It would be very interesting if some day someone managed to write a serious critical study about what it is exactly in a man that makes him want to become a soccer coach.
My own quite modest opinion is that if you want to do this job, as a professional or as an amateur, it makes little difference, what you need is a fairly good dose of masochism - you have to enjoy suffering. I can think of no other environment where ingratitude and the total lack of feeling reign so freely as in soccer.

THE FIRST STEP: PROGRAMS

At the very beginning the coach will have to draw up a technical, tactical behavioral and organizational program with his club, almost always represented in the person of his Coaching Director.
Your ideas and his will need to match as closely as possible, and you will have to work out together the general targets that you

are going for, after having made a careful evaluation of the quality of the players in the club.

At this point a list will be compiled including the players to be confirmed and those to be acquired in accordance with the coach's tactical ideas and experience. In cases where it proves absolutely impossible for the club to act on his requests, the coach will be forced to revise and correct them, just as he will have to take another look at the programs he has established.

THE 4-4-2 SYSTEM:
ADVANTAGES AND DISADVANTAGES

Zonal play can be put into effect with various systems, but we will be looking at the 4-4-2; though, keeping in mind that there is also a keeper on the field, the 4-4-2 should really be called a 1-4-4-2. This sort of code describing the placement of the players is called the basic numerical system: the first number indicates the defenders (4), the second indicates the mid fielders (4) and the third the strikers (2).

During the many phases of a match, the initial set up of the three lines (four man defense, four man mid field and two strikers) will undergo continuous variation, so that in the build up or the attacking phase (when our team is in possession) the system could turn into a 4-2-4, a 3-4-3 or a 3-4-1-2, a 3-3-1-3, etc. In the defense phase (when we are not in possession) the team could become a 5-3-2, a 5-4-1, a 4-4-1-1, etc.

It goes without saying that, like all playing systems, the 4-4-2 has advantages and disadvantages.

Advantages

1. The load of work is lighter because the players are not placed on the field in relation to their opponents but in relation to the ball.

2. The team must be 'short' (between the defender nearest to his own goal and the striker nearest to the opponents', there should never be more than 35 - 40 yards). With the three sections playing close together and because the opposition will have less space to play in, we will find it easier to regain possession.

3.   As we are playing with a 'short' team both in the defense and in the attacking phase, it is easier for us, on regaining possession, to bring even our mid fielders and our defenders to a position where they can shoot on goal.
4.   The reduced spaces between players allow for short passes and dump shots that are fairly easy to carry out.

Disadvantages

1.   We will have objective difficulty getting past our opponents as we go from zone to zone of the field.
2.   As we will be having less contact with our opponents, we need greater organization and this means that we have to concentrate from the beginning of the match to the end.
3.   When we are in possession we will be playing with our various sections in line; it is difficult to form triangles between players and that means the build up will be elaborate but slow.

THE 4-4-2 SYSTEM: PRESSING AND OFFSIDE AS ESSENTIAL REQUIREMENTS

Pressing and offside are the fundamental supports for playing an effective zonal 4-4-2. These are the characteristics that such a team will need to be enacting for the whole of the 90 minutes:

1.   Short team. The various sections will be playing close together.
2.   Interchange of roles. If need be every player will have to be able to carry out different roles even during the same match.
3.   Shorten up and tighten the opposition's playing space as soon as they get near the penalty area.
4.   Lengthen out and widen the opposition's ranks the moment we regain possession.
5.   Develop attacking plays that foresee the defenders and mid fielders breaking into the lines - these will have been codified and studied during training sessions.
6.   We will need to carry out tactical fouls so as to stop our adversary's counterattacks when our own team is off bal-

ance and too far forward. Mid fielders or strikers will have to commit this type of foul, which will often be followed by a booking.

Keeping in mind that this system requires zonal play, we will start by having a good look at the two fundamental supports of our play: pressing and offside.

Pressing

Pressing is an action made by two or more players (from the same or different sections of the team), which they carry out in order to reduce their opponent's playing space and time.
As soon as players go into pressing their team mates furthest away from the ball must get into a position that will allow them to anticipate their opponents. Players will probably not be able to carry out pressing for the whole length of the match, and so the coach must be able to get his team to apply it in the best way and at the right moment.
Good pressing can be carried out when an opponent:

1.   makes a mistake stopping the ball;
2.   looks down as he is about to kick;
3.   receives the ball along the sidelines;
4.   receives a long high ball from the back;
5.   receives a ball with his back turned to his opponent's goal;
6.   advances with the ball at his feet or insists in a personal action.

Pressing can be carried out in-depth, in the mid field or in defense. Where you decide to start pressing depends on a number or variables:

1.   your position in the standings;
2.   environmental situation (home or away matches);
3.   the conditions on the playing field;
4.   the score of the match;
5.   the playing time remaining;
6.   the psycho-physical condition of the team.

Invited pressing

Invited pressing is a pressing action that we do not carry out in a particular part of the playing field but against an opponent who we feel is in difficulty or is not playing well 'on the day'. We use special techniques that will allow him to come easily into possession and then we attack him.

Offside

By carrying out pressing in the right way and with the correct timing, we will often put our opponents into an offside position without even trying to - because the one is an offshoot of the other. At the moment of writing (2001 / 2002 season) offside is considered a foul when between the player who is on the point of receiving the ball and the goal line there are not at least two opponents, whatever their role in the team.
The player is not in an irregular position if he is in line (or when a part of his body is covered by the defenders furthest away from him) at the precise moment in which his attacking team mate kicks the ball to him so that he can have a shot at goal.
As we have said, even in cases where it is not carried out on purpose, offside is a logical consequence of pressing. There are, however, a couple of exceptions:

1.   the tactic can be carried out when the opposing goalkeeper puts the ball back into play with a long pass. The whole team sprints into depth in a coordinated way to limit problems that could come about when the keeper's long balls arrive almost to the edge of the penalty area.
2.   when the opposition includes specialists in aerial play and is about to take a free kick that will arrive ¾ down the field. The defenders can attract the attacking players into the penalty area and then, the moment the player on the ball is about to kick, the whole defense section sprints up field, leaving the opponents in an offside position.

There are risks, naturally, in applying offside in the situations I have just described, but it is also true that our opponents will find themselves in clear psychological difficulty in those specific episodes of play.

From the end of the eighties to the mid nineties hundreds of coaches, in serie A but also in amateur teams, 'monkeyed' these tactics taking them to ridiculous lengths. This resulted not only in matches that were a lot less spectacular, but it also made things very difficult for referees and their assistants.

In time, careful studies made by good coaches, and the counter-moves that they have brought to bear - coupled with modifications to the rules put into effect by the international federation - have ended up by creating a situation where the offside rule is applied with much greater economy in the soccer of today.

Many coaches have begun to feel that the risks inherent in the systematic application of offside tactics are greater than their benefits, and they now try to put them into practice only when the team is in a situation of numerical inferiority.

The defense elastic

The defense elastic is a tactic devised to create difficulty for the opposing team who are in the attacking phase. It can be carried out by a single defender (a center or a side back lying low, who, by shifting backwards, takes up the position of a sweeper), or by the whole defense line. Depending on the situation (and this is something that will have to be addressed again and again in training), and keeping a careful eye on the opponent's position (is he being pressed or is he free to make for the line of backs) the whole defense section, having been given the signal by their leader, should be able, on moving back, to place themselves in a straight line, in a diagonal or in triangular formation with its apex towards their goal. Once the defense line has intercepted the ball or made a long pass, it should immediately move up as a whole and go into depth to attack the ball, shortening the team, and, if possible, leaving the opponents in an offside position.

In cases where the ball is then intercepted by an opponent who might create a danger, the defenders carry out the elastic movement once again, going back this time in order to gain time and remove the opposing striker's in-depth space.

THE 4-4-2 SYSTEM: ITS CHARACTERISTICS

Defense

In this system there are four players in the defense line. Apart from giving the team good placement on the playing field, this also means that we will have the right coverage in the defense phase.

The four players must be closely knit: a single error in the group could easily lead to serious problems for their team. Of the four that make up the defense, two will be the side players (also called the right and the left side backs) and two the center players: the right and left center backs.

The side backs will have to defend, but, when called upon to do so, they will also have to move up during the attacking phase, and they will need the classic abilities of backs that can turn into attacking players. In the attacking phase these players must be fast, and they must be able to cross as well. Tactical intelligence is another essential requirement in order to be able to guide the timing and the direction of play even when they are not actually in possession.

The center defenders need to be compatible. One of them must be good in the air, and will need to be a big and powerful player; the other, physically forceful as well, must make the most of his speed.

A four man defense is impenetrable when organized to perfection and made up of players that are individually capable and whose characteristics are interrelated.

The mid field

Playing with a 4-4-2 you can place the mid field section in many different ways. Everything will depend on the coach's own ideas and the strengths and weaknesses of the players he has on hand. In particular, we can choose between:

1.   An in-line set up, with two center and two side mid fielders;
2.   The 'rhombus' placement, with a mid fielder shielding the

defense (low apex) or with an attacking mid fielder (in-depth apex) and two internal mid fielders

Looking at an in-line mid field (Fig 1.1) we need two center and two side mid players.
One of the two center mid fielders is very often the team leader; the other is his 'shield bearer', working as a sort of dam - i.e., able to cover his team mate, to attack the ball and set up the counter attacks.

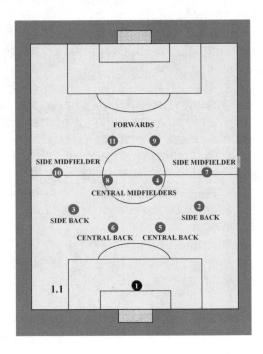

The attacking mid fielder must be:

1.   tactically skilled;
2.   technically skilled;
3.   physically strong;
4.   able to direct the team's timing of play;
5.   psychologically strong (with the personality of the leader);
6.   able to help out the defense when need be, and know how to time his plays as he breaks in during the attacking phase.

The second center mid fielder is always considered the man of bulk in the mid field, the one who can on occasion even mark the opposing attacking mid fielder. He will need to have the following characteristics:

1.　　physical strength;
2.　　temperament;
3.　　spirit of sacrifice;
4.　　tackling ability;
5.　　ability to overlap in the attacking phase and to double up in the defense phase;
6.　　aerial skills;
7.　　aerobic stamina;
8.　　technical skills, above all in the way he manages recovered balls.

The two side players complete our four man mid field section. These players will normally have attacking inclinations. One of them will usually be good at playing along the sidelines, at coming out on top in one to one situations so that he can cross the ball. The other is usually called a semi-striker: he gets round the defense and filters in inviting passes to the strikers.

The side mid fielder, sometimes known as the 'running' side mid fielder needs these characteristics:

1.　　good speed;
2.　　good dribbling;
3.　　tactical intelligence;
4.　　physical strength;
5.　　tackling ability;
6.　　ability to cross while he is on the run;
7.　　aerial ability;
8.　　he must be a potential goal scorer;
9.　　aerobic stamina and good at sudden changes in speed.

The second side mid fielder is at the same time the delight of every coach - and the thorn in his side. With one of his fantastic moves he can suddenly resolve even the most difficult of matches; but he can also disappear at times so completely from the play that it almost feels as if you had one man less on the field. With his dazzling technique this type of player can destroy the exasperating tactical play carried out by almost every team in modern soccer, and for that very reason his role would seem to be coming back into fashion after years of controversy and contention.

These are his characteristics:

1.   able to get round his opponent with disarming ease;
2.   technical ability well above the average;
3.   able to pass the ball at the right moment and to the right player;
4.   very good at 'creating' penalties and direct free kicks at the edge of the penalty area
5.   very good at kicking penalties and free kicks;
6.   good at shooting at goal even from far off.

As you will see, we have made no mention of his physical requirements. These are certainly not the central thing as regards the attacking mid fielder.
However, many coaches do not like this type of player, preferring muscular power to bolster the team's defense over sporadic offensive brilliance.

When the mid field section is lined up as a 'rhombus', we have players with complementary characteristics placed at each of its two apexes. At the lower apex (center mid fielder) you will need a player with tactical sense able to recover a large number of balls, and the player at its upper apex ('creative' or finishing touch player) will be feeding the strikers or dribbling and having a shot at goal. The two side mid fielders will be universal players - as active as possible and good during the two phases of play.

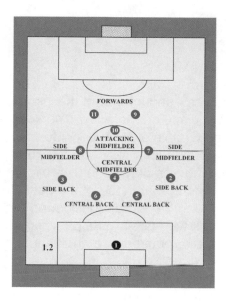

The attack

In front the two strikers can place themselves in line or with one (the second striker) behind the other - this will depend on the characteristics of each and on how those characteristics interact. The second of the two solutions will also allow you to bring a striker a few yards back, giving him the chance to play between the opponent's defense line and their mid field, in an area that will make him difficult for the defending team to manage. It goes without saying however, that if you want to place your strikers 'vertically', the two players will need to have particular character- istics so as not to undermine their effectiveness in attack. It would be a mistake to bring a player back and put him to work in the zone between the lines if he is not able, in fact, to turn round with the ball or to insert himself with the right timing when his point of reference cuts in a dump and rebound pass. Also, it could also be detrimental to put the strikers in a vertical system if the first striker is not particularly able to attack in-depth, and the second striker is not fast enough to go after him breaking in effectively with cutting passes.

THE 4-4-2 SYSTEM: PLAYER SPECIFICATIONS

The goalkeeper

Perhaps we never speak enough about this player, considering the importance of his place on the team. The keeper's way of playing has changed completely and become much more complicated down the years, and as a result of new rules and new playing systems, so that modern players in this role need characteristics that are very different from those of the past. Today almost all teams use the zone, and therefore, considering that the two supporting columns of this type of play are pressing and offside, the particular characteristics required of a goalkeeper are:

1. physical size;
2. great personality, allowing him not only to give his team mates a sense security and confidence in the critical moments of the match, but also making it easy for him to command the various movements of the defense;
3. readiness to move up when the team is carrying out in-depth pressing; at these times he will take up the position of the sweeper;
4. ability to use, if possible, both feet - keeping in mind that his long passes can give rise to the whole attacking move;
5. speed and determination when he comes out for high or low balls and when he is in a one to one situation.

Modern soccer expects players to exploit the sidelines, from where they will be able to cross the ball in the attempt to catch the defense unawares - and that is why it is an advantage for a team to have a keeper who is good at moving out. Even if you are not applying offside in a systematic way, it can often happen that the keeper will find himself in a one to one situation, and in such cases his speed, his ability to read the moment and his determination will all be vital to the result.

No matter how capable and proficient a goalkeeper may be between the posts he will be of little use to a team using zonal play if he is not good with his feet or if he is afraid when he has to come out of his goal.

The side defenders

The side defenders, even if they are placed for the most part in the defense zone, need also to have other abilities, in that they will be expected to play in the mid field so that they can help the mid fielders to build up play, and also in attack during the offense phase. Keeping these considerations in mind, their characteristics will be the following.

1.   ability to anticipate;
2.   running speed;
3.   tackling;
4.   jumping ability;
5.   speed in moving over short spaces;
6.   a good knowledge of the kind of movements required by a zonal defense;
7.   ability in taking up the right position for marking;
8.   able to carry out long and short diagonal passes
9.   able to double up;
10.   good at applying offside tactics;
11.   able to carry out quick overlapping;
12.   good at the one to one in attack;
13.   good at crossing,

The center defenders

These players are the last barrier beyond which the opponents can conclude their offensive action. Even if their philosophy and their way of playing has changed in time, the basics have remained the same: they are still the ultimate defenders. The center backs must be able to compensate for each other. One of the two will need these characteristics:

1.   physical size;
2.   good jumping ability;
3.   strength; ability to mark the opponent's first striker even in reduced space;
4.   must be determined and keep up his concentration for the whole match;
5.   must know the movements of the defense pyramid by heart.

The other center defender will not necessarily need to have the sheer physical size of the first. However, he will have to counter-balance his section team mate's characteristics with other quali-ties:

1.   speed;
2.   ability at clearing the ball in defense;
3.   ability to give orders about when to move into depth or to make defensive shifts (he must be a real leader in fact);
4.   ability to read the tactical situation on the field.

The center mid fielders (in-line mid field)

As we have already seen, with the basic 4-4-2 we can place the mid fielders either in-line or with a rhombus formation.
When the mid field section is in line here are the main requisites for one of the two center players:

1.   very good at tackling;
2.   good jumping ability;
3.   good at playing for time;
4.   tactical intelligence;
5.   drive;
6.   able if need be to mark the man - the opponent's attack-ing mid fielder;
7.   ability to integrate himself in the defense line;
8.   a sense of timing when carrying out rapid attacks.

The other center mid fielder will have to:

1.   be a good runner;
2.   be good at counterattacking;
3.   have good technique;
4.   be tactically expert;
5.   be good at making long passes and shooting from a distance,
6.   be capable during the championship to score some goals

Practically speaking, one of the two center mid fielders should be able to give constant balance to the defense, the other the attack; the first should be good at tackling, the other at running, organizing play and shooting, particularly during the transition phase.

The side mid fielders

In the 4-4-2, the side mid fielders play a delicate role. They are the ones, in fact, who, with their covering or supporting movements, make the team take up a defensive or attacking attitude depending on the situation.
Here again, the attitude and the requirements of the players will depend on whether the mid field is playing in-line or with a rhombus formation.

When the line-up calls for the two side mid fielders to be placed in depth and wide, these are the requirements for one of the two:

1.   ability in the two phases of play: the defense phase and the attacking phase;
2.   good running ability;
3.   excellent stamina;
4.   ability at getting round the opponent;
5.   ability at crossing from the opponent's back line;
6.   tactical ability; good goal scoring averages.

The other side mid fielder will need aptitudes that are slightly different from those of his team mate in the same section.
If one of them has marked attacking talent, the other will have to have a strong inclination for defense. He will need:

1.   good running stamina;
2.   good defensive doubling up skills;
3.   good tackling ability;
4.   selflessness;
5.   tactical intelligence.

In planning a match, coaches rarely use two side mid fielders with the same characteristics of play, unless of course they are adopting a different system (i.e., the 4-3-3).

Generally speaking the side mid fielders should be correspondent to the side defenders. The more attacking side mid fielder will be placed in control of the part of the field where the more defensive side mid fielder is stationed and vice versa.

The mid fielders in the rhombus lineup

There is, as we have seen, another way of using the mid fielders in the 4-4-2: the so called 'rhombus mid field'.

In this case, the placement of the four mid fielders is very different from that foreseen when they are playing in line. Clearly, therefore, in a section put on the field in this formation, the characteristics required of the players will be different, at least in part, from a mid field with two center players and two others playing wide and in depth.

The rhombus formation gives us two horizontal apexes formed by mid fielders whose location (at least at the start of the match) will be more centralized than the position assumed by those playing in line. The vertical apexes will be formed by mid fielders with well-defined characteristics: the lower apex will be taken by a defending mid fielder, good at contrasting and able to organize playing tempo; the in-depth apex will be what we call the 'creative' player, creating assists and going for a shot on goal.

The player on the lower apex will need:

1.   good technical skills;
2.   efficient tackling ability;
3.   strong personality;
4.   to be able to use both feet;
5.   to be able to organize the team's tempo;
6.   to be able to give orders concerning his section team mates' movements;
7.   good tactical ability.

The player occupying the in depth apex of the rhombus will usually be a 'creative' player who can also be used, when need be, as a second striker. He must be:

1.	of a high technical level;
2.	able to protect the ball so as allow the team to move into depth;
3.	able to create assists;
4.	good at shooting at goal even from a distance;
5.	good at dribbling;
6.	good at exchanging passes and then shooting at goal himself;
7.	good at 'creating' fouls just outside the penalty area.

One of the horizontal apexes of the rhombus will have to be a mid fielder with these characteristics:

1.	good at tackling;
2.	able to give support to attacking play;
3.	very good tactical skills;
4.	marked aptitudes in defense and construction;
5.	able to double up on opponents in possession;
6.	able to overlap when the team is counterattacking;
7.	good in the transition phase.

Positioned at the other horizontal apex of the rhombus we will have a player who is:

1.	good at constructing play;
2.	good at dribbling;
3.	good basic speed;
4.	good at crossing as he is running with the ball;
5.	able to defend and protect the ball;
6.	good at shooting even from far out;
7.	good elevation;
8.	good in the transition phase.

The transition phase is when you go from attacking to defense play or vice versa. Players who can occupy the most suitable areas of the field as quickly as possible during these phases are said to be in possession of good tactical ability.

The strikers

In a boxing match where everything depends on points the better boxer will be the one to win; in basketball the team with the better players nearly always comes out on top - in soccer the winner is the team that has scored the most goals. Take a look at the 'soccer market', and what you are watching is the desperate search for the rarest of goods - the strikers, players who can make or break a club or its coach. In our imagination they are our heroes, sometimes even managing to make a whole city jump for joy at one touch of the ball. They are loved and criticized, their life depends on an inch or two, in or wide, aces or asses, everything and its opposite. These are the strikers.

In the 4-4-2 system we normally use two complementary strikers: the first of the two will be powerful and physically imposing; the second more mobile.

These are the characteristics of the first striker:

1.   physical strength;
2.   elevation;
3.   great ability to protect the ball;
4.   good shot at goal with one of his feet at least;
5.   goal sense, opportunist;
6.   good acrobatic ability;
7.   willing to sacrifice himself.

These are the characteristics of the second striker.

1.   great ability to move around and attack any space;
2.   able to get past his opponent;
3.   intensity of play;
4.   good at shooting from a distance;
5.   good elevation;
6.   good running stamina;
7.   drive;
8.   altruism

These are more or less what the coach will be looking for in the two strikers of the 4-4-2. Of course, in cases where the team as a whole does not include players with these characteristics the coach will have to make do with what he has and look for other solutions.

From this analysis one thing is clear, and we can conclude by saying that in order to put a certain system into practice the coach will have to have clear ideas on how to do so, but he also needs to have the players who can interpret it.

CHAPTER 2

TEACHING THE DEFENSE PHASE

Marco Ceccomori

PREFACE

The defense phase can be defined as the collective tactical situation facing a team when their opponents are in possession. Along with the attacking phase and the transition phase, it is one of the three fundamental phases in the game of soccer.
It goes without saying that your prime aim in the defense phase is to make sure that the opposition do not score a goal against you.
However, to limit the whole defense strategy to that alone will appear much too trite and superficial. Modern soccer has reached a high level of tactical organization as a natural consequence of its aim to have a suitably predisposed group of players and a defensive outlook that is **ACTIVE** and **RESOURCEFUL**.
This can only come about by creating collaborative playing mechanisms tending towards an effective and valid reconquest of ball possession.
Putting such mechanisms into effect requires making strategic choices, and these will be the result of the obvious connection that exists between the two phases of non possession and possession.
The way you regain possession (intercepting, tackling or as a result of your opponents' fouls) and the part of the field in which this actually takes place will determine the development of your attacking moves.
If, for example, our team gets possession near our penalty area, we will naturally have a long way to go before arriving at our opponent's goal, and we will therefore have to build up our play from far back, running the risk of losing the ball in a dangerous area; either that, or we will have to go for a long pass, with the difficulties such a choice creates for our strikers. High level defensive organization is, therefore, a basic foundation for success. And even the most attack-minded coaches would agree with that.
If a team is forever allowing goals, it will never be able to win anything important even if its own goal scoring averages are high.
An organized and effective playing system which makes it difficult for the opponents to score will bring a sense of security and morale to the whole team, giving the attacking phase the neces-

sary continuity, fluidity and unpredictability.

The coach must be good at observing, evaluating and searching out the technical, tactical, physical, athletic and psychological attitudes of his players with the aim of choosing the playing system and the defense strategy that is most suitable for his group.

Soccer is a situational sport, and in training the coach must know how to get over to his players those procedures that will enable them to read and interpret the various situations that will come about on the field. The players' reactions must be adequate to the defensive strategy of the team and to the two most important variables in the game of soccer: **SPACE** and **TIME**.

The less space and time we leave to our opponents, the more difficult it will be for them to get a chance to shoot at goal.

Apart from these technical and tactical aspects, another vital element that needs to be looked into in order to improve the phase of non-possession is our defensive mentality - our mental approach and predisposition to defending.

Determination, intensity, clear-sightedness, intelligence, aggressiveness - these are just some of the numerous qualities that must be part of the DNA of a good player working in defense, along with a marked ability to anticipate, by which is meant capacity to foresee how play will develop. This last is an essential condition of modern soccer because of its speed and because of the limited space in which you now have to play.

TEACHING METHODS

In zonal play each player is responsible for the part of the field assigned to him, and for the opponents who enter there.
A player not in possession must also control the nearby zones and contrast any opponent entering his zone with the ball.
In order to reach the best possible **organization of the defense phase** following zonal principles the coach should underline the main concepts to be referred to, in this order: **the ball, the team mates and the opponents**.
A well-organized team will move in a way that is both coordinated (i.e., with the right timing) and compact (keeping short and close together), and the players will do so in association with the movements of the **ball** and in relation to the position of the **team mates** and the **opponents**, respecting the distances between the sections of the team and the players in each single section.
The principle aim is to create **numerical superiority** around the ball. The team becomes more compact close to the ball, where the nearest opponents will be tightly marked and the ball covered (i.e., pressed), while other players are trying at the same time to anticipate opponents further away and to intercept the passes in their direction.
In all he says or makes them do, the coach should be trying to get his players to 'think and act collectively', in the attempt to prepare the team so that they are in a position to 'read' the various playing situations in a uniform way.
In essence, there are **five basic collective tactical principles** that a team involved in the phase of non-possession will have to respect::

1. **ranking:** not to place yourself on the field in a fixed or even formation, but creating various lines of coverage;
2. **playing for time:** slowing down the opponents' play in certain situations, as when there is incorrect placement of the team on the field, numerical inferiority, dynamic or athletic difficulties due to tiredness which make it hard to attack the ball, etc.;
3. **defensive concentration:** closing up and restricting playing space so as to create greater difficulties for the opponents;

4.   **defensive balance:** attempting to create numerical superi
ority in all zones of the field;

5.   **aggressiveness:** continuous pressing on the player in
possession and his supporting team mates in order to
restrict his playing space and time.

The teaching methods to be followed in order to reach good playing organization can be divided into four phases:

1   defining the individual's technical / tactical tasks by carrying out simple exercises without an opponent or with a
passive or semi-active opponent - here the aim is the
separate construction of the various sections of the team;

2   instruction and more complicated exercises for the
defense line with active opponents;

3   exercises tending towards the integration of the mid field
section with the defense in order to reach block strategy;

4   collective exercises with the insertion of the attack playing
with the defense- mid field block; defining the team
strategy.

We must add that the various stages shown above do not necessarily have to follow one upon the other in a categorical or rigid
way. The careful examination of the training sessions and above
all the matches (which are always the best exam) will give the
coach a good idea of the level of organization reached by the
team, thus enabling him to choose the best exercises to carry out
in order to get over any problems that may have come up.

THE ZONAL 4-4-2

As you can see in Fig 2.1, the zonal 4-4-2 is distinguished by the
presence of four in line defenders, four in line mid fielders and
two strikers.
Rather that using the term 'in line' it would be more correct when
speaking about the defense and the mid field to talk about their
placement in a 'semi-circle' because the two side players take up
a position that is slightly advanced in relation to the others.
The 4-4-2 is probably the best system for effective defending

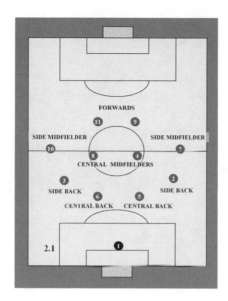

because the presence of two lines of four players in the defense and mid field sections enable you to cover the entire width of the field from right to left.

The team must be able to move compactly on the field remaining short and tight in reaction to the movements of the ball. This will favor a natural application of pressing and double teaming between the various chains of players.

THE DEFENSE

We have already said that the presence of four players in the defense line gives us good coverage of the entire width of the field.

After suitable coaching, the defense line should be able to move in a coordinated way in relation to the ball and with respect to the individual, section and collective tactical principles, protecting aggressively against rival strikers and trying to read the situations of play in the best way possible.

Besides this, from a mental point of view the defense section must concentrate and keep their attention up from start to finish. They must play at all times with conviction and confidence, fully aware that one error could be fatal to the result.

Individually speaking, the two **side defenders** must cover the sidelines and, using the diagonal, tighten in towards the center of the field when the ball is on the opposite sideline, being careful not to let themselves be taken by surprise on the weak side or in the blind zone. In addition, they will be marking the opposing side players - just how tightly will depend on the zone of the field and the position of the ball - and must try not to be passed in the one against one, anticipating, playing for time, shortening up on the opponent with the right timing and choosing the right moment for their intervention.

The two **center defenders** will be controlling the central zone of the defense, covering each other and giving coverage to the nearest side player, marking the opposing center strikers, being good in the air and as good as the side defenders in the one against one.

The opponent should be met sideways, never frontally. This principle applies to defenders, but also to mid fielders and strikers. This means that it is important to focus on the position of the defender's body and his feet (normally the inside foot will be in front of the outside foot, which will in turn be in line with the direction in which the ball is moving).

For the best defensive organization we should take a special look at a number of fundamental concepts:

1.   width;
2.   defensive diagonals and triangles;
3.   marking and covering;
4.   horizontal movements and section doubling up;
5.   vertical movements.

WIDTH

When the opponents are in possession, the defense section will have to place themselves tightly on the field (forty yards at most) reducing the intervening spaces between the players.

The defensive line will be more or less spaced out on the field depending on where exactly it is placed. As you get nearer to the goal to be defended, the distance between the players will get progressively less.

Another thing that will condition any variation in the width of the defense line is the number of opposing strikers and their placement on the field. Against a rival team lined up with two central strikers our defense line will be tighter than when we are playing against three strikers (a center forward and two wings playing wide). We will be having a look later at how to respect such principles of covering and marking.

EXERCISE 1

Width of the defense. (Fig. 2.2)
You place the defense line at the three quarters mark with two opponents set out in front of the two side backs. An adversary on the side attacks the defense with the ball. The defenders attack the ball and accompany the player without intervening, slipping backwards and restricting space as they get nearer to the area.

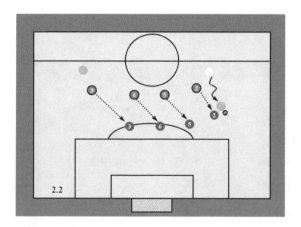

DEFENSIVE DIAGONALS AND TRIANGLES

The diagonal and the triangle are the two fundamental principles of zonal play. With an external ball the defense must close up on the ball, setting themselves in diagonal configuration, forming one or two lines of coverage depending on the coach's strategic decisions. A four man row placed to form a single line of coverage (Fig. 2.3) reduces the opponent's depth and makes it easier to use passive or active offside tactics.

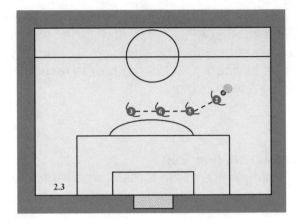

2.3

The decision to use a double line of coverage, with the two center defenders covering each other gives us more protection while conceding greater depth and making it more difficult to carry out offside tactics.

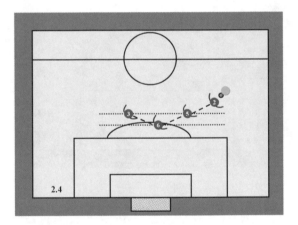

2.4

There are two ways of setting up the double covering line. The first is the so called 'L-shaped' or 'curved' defense with the side back opposite to the ball taking up position in line with the center defender who is nearest to the ball (Fig. 2.4). In the second, the side back furthest from the ball puts himself in line with the center back nearest to him. (Fig. 2.5).

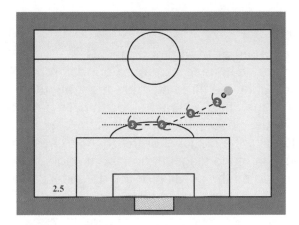

The basic difference between these two ways of setting out the double line of coverage is that with the first you are better positioned for good play in the transition, because, with the opposite side back in front, he will be ready to move into depth should the team regain possession.

If you have tactically skilled players on the team, I would personally tell them to defend with a single covering line on a covered ball and a double line on uncovered balls so as to get full advantage from the two ways of using the line.

With a central ball the four players need to place themselves as a triangle. The central defender in whose zone the ball has entered will be attacking it, the others tightening in to create the defensive triangle or pyramid (Fig. 2.6).

The diagonal and the triangle are defensive movements to be used both when the ball is on the **ground** and in the **air**.

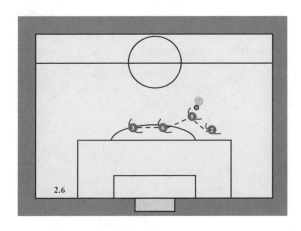

EXERCISE 2

Forming diagonals or triangles (Fig. 2.7).
The defense is placed near the area. Four different colored cones will be put on the three quarters mark about ten yards apart one from the other. When the coach calls out a color the defense line must close quickly in on the corresponding point of reference, forming the diagonal or the triangle. Apart from the correct execution of the diagonal and the triangle, the coach must also keep an eye on the position of the defenders' feet and body.

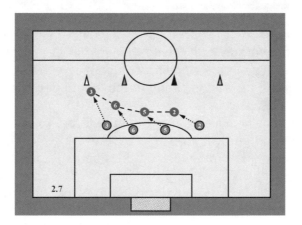

EXERCISE 3

Forming diagonals and triangles. (Fig. 2.8)
The defense is positioned as in the last exercise. In place of the cones there are now four players with a ball. When the coach gives his signal, the four players will start passing the ball around, attacked by the defense. At the start the ball will move following the coach's indications, then at the players' discretion.

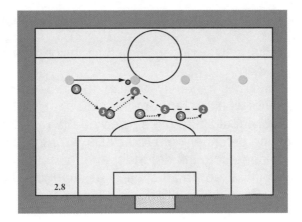

EXERCISE 4

Passing the ball around the defense
This exercise, though it is principally connected with the attacking phase, is very useful for the defense phase as well. The four defenders must pass the ball around, following each pass by moving into a diagonal position to give support to the team mate that receives. This coaches how to cover your nearby team mate and how to respect distances between players.

MARKING AND COVERING

The defensive movements that we have been looking at (the diagonal and the triangle) do not call for adversaries.
It is very important to point out that the presence of opponents can force the defenders to change position in order to respect the principles of marking, above all, as we will see in a moment, in some parts of the field and in certain situations.
Defenders using zonal play must be good at placing themselves on the field in such a way as to carry out two things correctly and at the same time: **marking and covering**.
In other words, in zonal play the defender cannot limit himself to controlling the opponent who enters his zone, but must place himself in such a way as to give coverage to a nearby section team mate, so that he can intervene at once on the ball should an opponent manage to get round a player next to him.
This is a very important concept for the success of the defense phase because a player who knows he is being covered by a

team mate will play more naturally and confidently, creating more initiatives.

To better understand this concept we can consider the principle of 'T-shaped marking'.

This type of marking is generally applied on the weak side against opponents who are far from the ball.

The 'T' is a **theoretical** figure used to divide the part of the field that separates the defender from the striker in order to show the part of the field nearest to the defender and the part nearest to the striker. With this **theoretical** system we mark out the defender's possible points of intervention and closure on the striker. Practically speaking, the player involved in defense must succeed in intervening on the striker and in closing off his direct adversary who has received the ball before he can shoot from a position favorable to him and thus in our danger zone. In Fig 2.9 and 2.10 we are looking at the 'T' marking of two players on their direct adversaries. In the first case, the defender's position - and thus his marking - is correct because the line of intervention and closure is outside the danger zone.

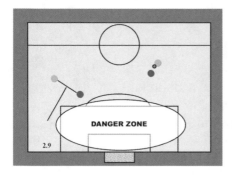 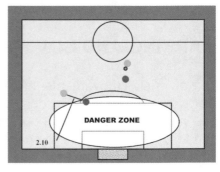

In the second case the marking is not very good because the line of intervention and closure is inside the danger zone.

'T' marking is very important to establish the position the defender must take up to carry out his two tasks: marking and covering. (Fig. 2.11).

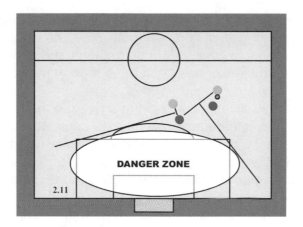

As far as the defense section goes, we can say that in cases where a defending player is unable to both mark and cover, he can be helped in carrying out both these tasks by the team mate nearest to him. Even while the latter is in turn engaged in marking, he can very often place himself in such a way as to be able to close in on the other's man. In order to decide if such a possibility exists in theory we must see if the defenders' lines of intervention and closure cross over outside the danger zone (Fig. 2.12).

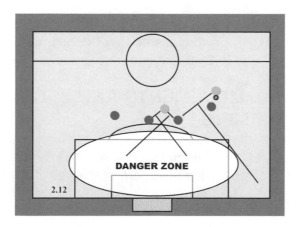

In cases where your team mate cannot help in controlling your opponent and you cannot carry out both your tasks (marking and covering), it is best to concentrate on marking and close on the ball only when the striker has beaten the team mate you were supposed to cover.

Another important thing is that, having arrived to the limit of its own penalty area, the defense will have to dedicate itself specifically to marking the opposing strikers. The nearer we get to our own goal the tighter marking should become - until in the end we are marking the man (leaving a single yard to the opponents can be fatal to the defense).

My advice is that an arm's length is the right distance between a defender and the striker he is marking inside the area.

EXERCISE 5

Forming diagonals and triangles in the presence of opponents.
As in exercises 2 and 3, but with the presence of progressively more strikers (from one to four). Give attention to the idea 'mark and cover'.

EXERCISE 6

As in exercise 1, bringing on 2 strikers. The player in possession arrives to the base line and crosses. Pay attention to the idea 'mark and cover' and to tight marking during a cross.

HORIZONTAL MOVEMENTS AND SECTION DOUBLE TEAMING

As we have already said the defense line must move in a coordinated way in relation to the movement of the ball in our opponent's possession. The four defending players must move horizontally with the correct timing, shortening up around the ball and maintaining the proper distances from each other.

Another thing that an organized defense needs is to know how to shift. This is a fundamental aspect of zonal play, closely connected to the covering and controlling functions of defenders, not only in their own zones but in adjacent zones.

What happens in a shifting move is that a section of the team (and in this case we are talking about the defense) slips over in a certain direction, so reorganizing the placement of the defense in what was a situation of numerical inferiority around the ball.
In cases where an opponent gets round a defender or when the back is out of position, the other defenders must respond to the new situation by shifting in relation to the ball, so applying the concept that any space left free by one player is occupied by a nearby team mate (Fig. 2.13).
Turning to doubling up inside the defense section, we must first underline the fact that doubling up must be carried out with great attention by defending players. Doubling up movements are risky because they free spaces for the opponents and can only be done in an organized way in defense, and after careful reading of the situation of play because they will almost always be taking place near the goal to be defended.

Generally speaking, we can distinguish two types of double teaming among defenders:

❒   doubling up from the sides towards the center;
❒   doubling up from the center towards the sides.

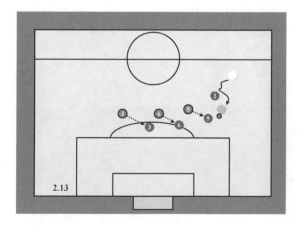

2.13

In the first case, the side back moves over to double up the marking on the center back nearest to him. Situations like this can come about for example when we are in the penalty area and an opponent controlled by the center defender, having received the ball, is just about to shoot; or if the striker being marked by the center back makes a movement to steer wide with the ball and the side back, having nobody to control, goes in to double up (Fig. 2.14).

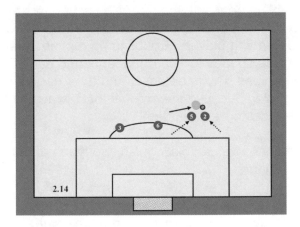

In the second case the center back goes to double up on the opponent marked by the side defender. A tactical decision like this can be made, for example, when the player in possession is very good in one to one situations and so we need to help the side back; or if the player in possession on the sidelines keeps the ball and delays his cross or if his back is turned (Fig. 2.15)

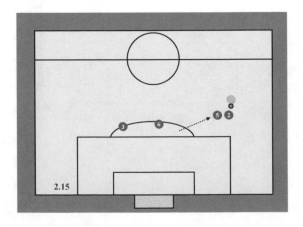

A tactical situation that is particularly interesting to look at, and which includes the principles of shifting, covering and doubling up, is when the side back finds himself above the line of the ball because he has been beaten by an opponent's dribbling or by a pass. In this case the side defender will have to make up his mind whether to double up the marking on the player in possession, who has now fallen under the control of the center defender shifting over to the side, or to go and take this team mate's place at the center (Fig. 2.16).

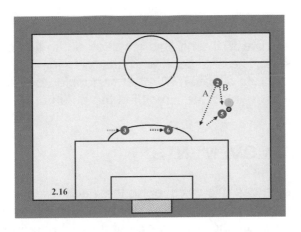

Decisions like this can only be taken after a careful reading of the situation on the field, keeping in mind the characteristics of the player in possession (to start with whether he is good at dribbling) and the placement of our defense in relation to the opposing strikers (look for any free spaces or gaps, think about numerical inferiority, etc.).

EXERCISE 7

Shifting movements in defense
The four backs pass the ball around as in exercise 4. When the coach gives the signal, the defender in possession becomes a striker and goes for the goal as the other members of the defense tighten in and shift in relation to the ball.

EXERCISE 8

An opponent in possession goes for the defense section from the side. The side defender under attack must accompany the player in possession, and, when the coach gives the signal, allow him to get past. The defense must then shift in relation to the ball, and the defender who has been sidestepped must choose between double teaming the player in possession or integrating with the defense section in a diagonal position to the ball.

EXERCISE 9

This exercise is like n° 8, only this time you put in first one, and then two strikers. The side back who has been jumped must decide in a concrete situation whether to double up on the player in possession or re integrate himself in the defense.

VERTICAL MOVEMENTS

Apart from being capable of covering the whole width of the field, the defense must be able to make effective vertical movements. The defense section should never be static, but should be carrying out correct vertical movements using the 'defense elastic'.
By defense elastic we mean those movements made during the defense phase by the backs as a section. Going into depth and pulling backwards in a coordinated way depending on the tactical situation, they have a double aim in mind. The first is to restrict the opponents' attacking depth and the second to shorten up the team, keeping the correct distance from the mid field.
The perfect movement of the defense elastic comes as a result of the four defenders' clear and uniform ability to grasp whether the ball is covered (when there is pressure on the ball, preventing precise passes into depth) or uncovered (there is no pressure on the ball and the opposing player in possession will be able to make a vertical pass undisturbed).
With an uncovered ball the defenders will have to move back quickly to get control of any possible in-depth pass from their opponents (Fig. 2.17). With a covered ball on the other hand, the defense must not 'run away'; rather, they should mark their oppo-

nents in an aggressive way and continue to move on up as we will see in detail in a moment, especially if they are using active offside tactics (Fig. 2.18).
As with the defense, so also the goalkeeper should also be trained to move up and back with the defense.

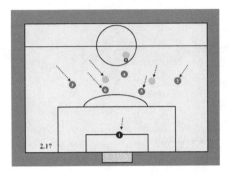 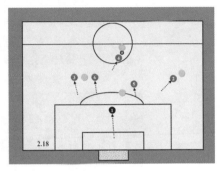

Other tactical situations in which the team should move back:

☐   numerical inferiority during an opponent's attack. You move back to slow down your adversary's play and to give your team mates time to get back into position. In such a situation the team's defense strategy might also foresee use of offside tactics;
☐   the defending team is badly placed on the field.

Tactical situations in which the team should move into depth:

☐   an opponent's back pass;
☐   player in possession with his back to the goal;
☐   when the defense has kicked the ball into depth.

How far back should the defense move when it is being attacked by an covered opponent? The four defenders should run back more or less to the crescent of the penalty area, at which point they should attack the player in possession using the diagonal with side balls and the triangle if it is central.

Two situations that deserve special mention are how to mark a striker that is running into depth and how to mark one moving up to receive a pass.

In the first case, unless the defense is coming out in the situations that we have already seen, the defender controlling a striker sprinting into depth should carry out a 'follow and quit' movement - i.e., accompany the opponent for a moment as he allows him to free himself of marking, and then move up again and get back into his section when the opponent is beyond the defense line and the pass has not yet been effected, thus leaving him offside (Fig. 2.19).

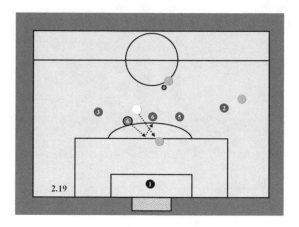

2.19

Another situation when the back should make a 'follow and quit' move is when the striker is going to meet a ball. He must accompany the striker's movement allowing him to get free of marking as he moves to a position where he can take a pass, returning to his original position if the striker does not actually receive the ball. Following an opponent who is moving to receive a pass is very important because it does not allow him to receive the ball free of pressure in an area between the defense line and the mid field. (Fig 2.20).

This last type of movement is very important even when the defense is moving backwards. Once again, the defender should follow the striker's movement to free himself of marking as he moves to take a pass, but this time the defense line will be moving back as well. A tactical solution of this type is to be carried out above all in cases of positive transition by the opponents because the follow and quit will allow you to mark and put pressure on the point of reference for the adversary in their counterattack.

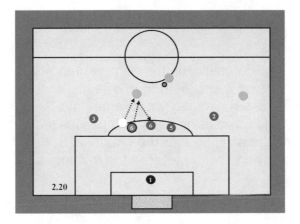

EXERCISE 10

Movements of the defense
The coach guides the ball in all directions with the defense moving in relation to it. Pay special attention to their grasp of covered or uncovered ball (Fig. 2.21)

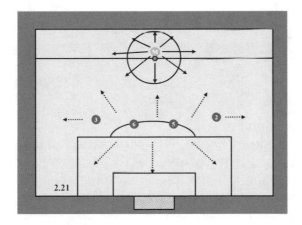

EXERCISE 11

The defense elastic

The defense is placed between the penalty area and the mid field line. A row of players faces them at mid field. The first player of this row makes for the defense (uncovered ball). After ten yards or so the player in possession turns and passes to the second with the defense moving up until the opponent is just about to control the ball. The second player in the row repeats the exercise (Fig. 2.22).

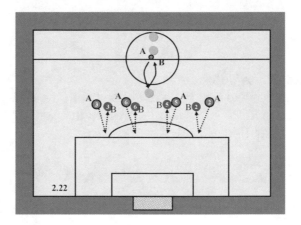

2.22

EXERCISE 12

The defense elastic

The defense is lined up near the outer crescent of the area. An opponent is placed centrally about ten yards from the mid field line. Standing to the side, the coach sends the ball to the defense who kick it away taking care of coverage. After clearing the ball, the defense then moves up until the opponent replays it into depth (Fig. 2.23).

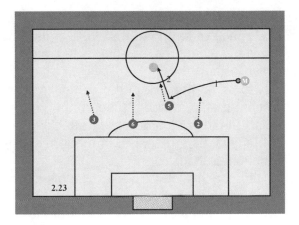

2.23

THE MID FIELD

Because it is made up of four players, the mid field of the 4-4-2 can cover the field in all its width in the best possible way.
From the point of view of their individual tactics, **the two central players** have a similar task. Basically, they act as a filter in front of the defense, protecting the central zone and trying to maintain their distance from the backs and to double up with the center defenders. Also, they must cover each other, placing themselves diagonally to the movement of the ball; when the opponents are attacking from the sides, they must cover the nearest side mid fielder or mark the supporting player next to the ball, depending on the situation. **The two side mid fielders** must protect space on the flanks or double up with the side backs. They must also tighten into the field creating the diagonal when the ball is on the opposite side, or even act as the fifth man of the defense depending on the position of the ball or of their team mates, on the opposition's line up or the defense strategy of the team as chosen by the coach.
The mid field needs to be well-trained in the principle movements or ideas of zonal play as have already been set out in relation to the defense line - the diagonal (in this case we will almost always be using a double covering line) the triangle and shifting movements.
One thing needs to be said, however: because it is placed further away from the goal to be defended than the defense section, the mid field will generally concentrate more on covering space rather than marking the opponents.

During the defense phase the main task of the center mid fielders is not to concede space or tempo to the opponents' plays; they will succeed in this by using pressure (individual action) and pressing (collective action).

In fact, our ability to be aggressive in the center of the mid field is not only a significant feature of the phase of non-possession; it can also be decisive in the outcome of our attacking phase - remember how many goals are scored in modern soccer as a result of sudden counterattacks.

For that reason, the coach's job is to exercise his mid field in the movements of pressing and individual pressure.

To my mind, the movement that is most important to train is the position the center mid fielder nearest to the ball should take up during an opposition's side attack.

The player in question has two options: he can cover the side mid fielder or he can go into anticipatory marking on a supporting player near the ball.

In order to make the best choice the center mid fielder must carefully review and judge the situation of play - most important of all, whether there is good coverage (covered ball) or not (uncovered ball) on the player in possession.

When the ball is covered the center mid fielder will carry out anticipatory marking on the nearby supporting player (Fig. 2.24); in the case of an uncovered ball, he will place himself diagonally (Fig. 2.25)

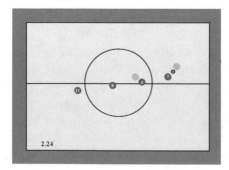
2.24

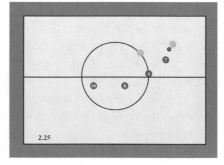
2.25

Also, the center mid fielder can double team with the side mid
fielder in tactical situations that can lead to greater aggressiveness on the ball (the player in possession has his back turned,
he controls the ball badly, he has to stop a pass coming high, he
is hugging the ball, the pass has been badly made). In cases like
these the whole mid field section should shift in relation to the
ball (Fig. 2.26).

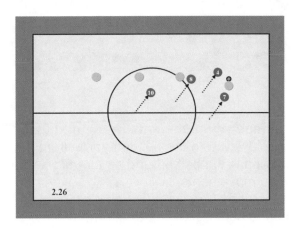

2.26

As concerns a central ball, the mid field will have to be more pru-
dent in its tactical choices because the opponent in possession
will be able to play around 360°, as distinct from the situation
when the ball is on the side (always remember that the sidelines
delimiting the field tend to play with the defense).
With central ball the mid field section will set up defensive triangles, unless, of course, we are in the presence of the various difficulties for the opposition that we have just spoken about, which
will lead to a more aggressive defensive attitude and so to doubling up the marking or anticipatory marking on the nearby supporting players. (Fig. 2.27).

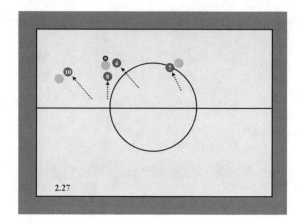

2.27

EXERCISE 13

Analysis of defensive movements in the mid field
You place four players with the ball ten yards from the mid field line. These four pass the ball around as the mid fielders carry out passive defense movements.

Depending what type of pressure is being brought on the player in possession, the center mid fielder alternates coverage of the nearby side mid fielder with marking the adjacent supporting player (cf.. Fig. 2.25 and 2.26 respectively). After a while the four players passing the ball will simulate at will any of the above mentioned tactical situations (e.g., they receive the ball and then turn their back to the goal) which can lead to more aggressive behavior in the defense. At this point, the mid fielders will carry out doubling up movements and will begin to mark the nearby supporting players (cf. Fig 2.26 and 2.27).

EXERCISE 14

Situation defensive movements in the mid field. (Fig 2.28)
In a 40 x 30 yd rectangle two mid field sections are lined up facing each other. Their aim is to get past the line in front while defending the line behind.

The movements of the preceding exercise are carried out in a situational context.

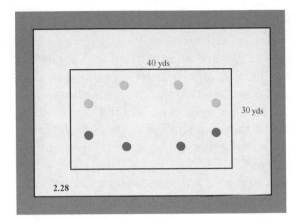

2.28

EXERCISE 15

4 vs. 4 vs. 4. (Fig 2.29)
You can use this exercise for the defense as well. In a field 40 x 50 yds. two teams of four players are facing each other with a free zone in the center. The blue and the red players are placed in the two halves and the black players with the ball in the free zone. The four players in possession attack one of the two teams (for example the blues) with the aim of getting past the line behind them. The team under attack must try to regain possession and, having done so, must kick it to the reds placed in the other half of the field who will send it straight back without controlling it to the blues who have followed up the pass. Now the reds have to defend the line behind as the blues attack them, and, on regaining possession, send it to the blacks in the other half, following up the pass, and so on.

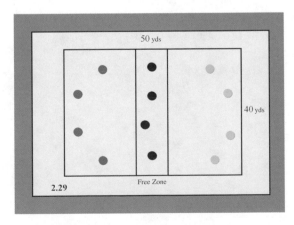

2.29

THE ATTACK

The two strikers also have an important role to play in the defense phase. I do not agree at all with those who claim that strikers should take no part in the defense phase because otherwise they will lose their freshness when it comes to shooting. The coach must make sure his strikers appreciate their importance to the phase of non-possession, convincing them that they must be the first defenders.

The two strikers must think and move in a coordinated way, respecting the distance from the mid field section and putting pressure on their opponents with the aim of either regaining possession in an advantageous position for their team or slowing down the opposition's plays so that their defense and mid field can get back into the best positions from which to carry out the defense phase.

The strikers must not let their opponents get round them too easily, but should force the opposing defenders to play onto the sidelines in order to create a strong side and a weak side, which will make it easier to set up good pressing.

In addition, they must double up on the mid fielders and mark any defenders that are supporting the counterattack.

EXERCISE 16

The two strikers in the defense phase
Three defenders and two strikers face each other in a rectangle 15 x 30 yds. placed at the center of one half of the field. The two strikers have to defend the line behind them and try to regain possession, after which they will move into depth and shoot at goal as the defenders close in on them.

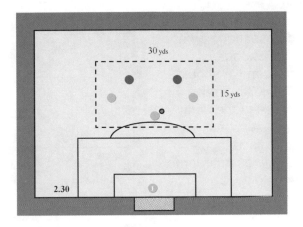

COLLECTIVE MOVEMENTS MADE BY THE 4-4-2 IN THE DEFENSE PHASE

We will now have a good look at the collective defense movements that the 4-4-2 must carry out in order to regain possession of the ball in an effective way. The following are the principle tactical defensive plays to be used with that end in view:

❏   Covering the spaces;
❏   Doubling up;
❏   Pressing;
❏   Offside

COVERING THE SPACES

As we have already seen, a team is said to be organized if it manages to move itself compactly and in a coordinated way in relation to the ball, keeping itself short and tightly-knit and respecting the distances between the sections and between the various players within each section.
The team must be able to align itself to the ball using 'T-shaped' marking against opponents placed on the weak side; and it must be able to mark as tightly as possible the supporting players near covered balls.
On the field this tactical attitude will ensure that the team is covering all the spaces in the best and the most rational way.
Covering the spaces is a very important defensive action leading

to regaining possession by intercepting a bad pass made by an opponent or a loose ball.

To arrive at this aim we should take care of the collaborative movements between the defense and the mid field sections, which should normally place themselves in zigzag lines in order to set up defense triangles.

The team must be shifting in the right way onto the flanks, and the side mid fielder must be good at integrating with the defense in certain tactical situations of play. As we have seen, in cases

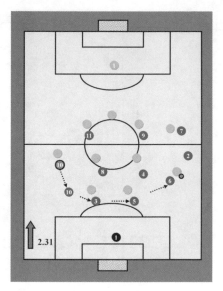

where our side defender has been sidestepped, or where he is out of position or has delayed in moving back, the other three defenders must shift and shorten in on the ball, while the side mid fielder opposite to the ball should join the defense on the weak side. (Fig. 2.31)

The side mid fielder can integrate himself in the defense even when it is correctly in position, creating what is called the fifth man in the defense.

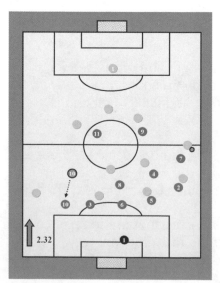

For example, when the defense is well back with the ball on the sidelines, the side mid fielder furthest from the development of play can unite with the defense, allowing the side back nearest to him to tighten in even more (Fig. 2.32).

We must point out, however, that any backward move made by the side mid fielder will be in inverse proportion to his function and incisiveness during positive transition. The further he moves back the greater the distance he will have to cover to get himself back into a position favorable for our counter attack.

It is important to know your side mid fielder's playing characteristics very well, so putting yourself in a position to expect defensive tasks from him that do not inhibit his attacking inclinations.

DOUBLE TEAMING

Doubling up is a defense action on the part of a player who goes to help a team mate who is already facing an opponent in possession - therefore creating a two against one situation.

We can make the following distinctions concerning the role of the player going in to double up with respect to his team mate who is marking the player in possession:

☐   section double teaming, which comes about when a player goes to help a team mate from his own section: this is a situation that we have already surveyed in detail when we were looking at the movements of the defense and the mid field;

☐   double teaming between players of different sections, which can be carried out by moving forwards or back wards.

We have forward doubling up when the player moves into depth to double team (Fig. 2.33)

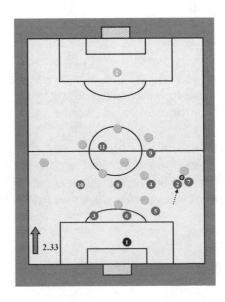

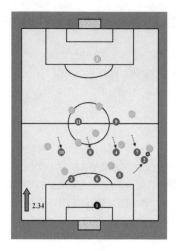 

Backward marking is more common, and this takes place when the player moves back because he is placed in advance with respect to the ball (Fig. 2.34).
It is to be noted that the player who is doubling up can himself regain possession, or position himself in such a way as to allow his team mate to get back the ball.

Generally speaking, the decision whether to carry out one or the other of the above mentioned actions will depend on the placement of the opponent in possession.
As an example let us imagine that the player in possession has his back to our goal, and doubling up is being carried out by a mid fielder moving back on an opponent contrasted by a defender: in such a case, the player going in to double up should intervene to take back the ball while his team mate is making sure that the opponent cannot turn around (Fig. 2.35).

When the opponent is facing our goal and we are making a backward doubling up move, the player doing the action should place himself internally to the opponent so that he can accompany him along the sideline and so favor the team mate's intervention.

PRESSING

Pressing is a collective defensive action aiming to limit the opponents' playing space and time. Pressure, on the other hand, is a defensive action by which a single player tries to reduce the space and time of an opponent who has entered his zone.
It follows therefore that, while there can be pressure without pressing, there can never be pressing without pressure on the player in possession. In order to carry out effective and well-organized pressing the team must be compact: the players must be correctly placed on the field, with the correct distances between the sections and between the components of each individual section. It helps if the team has an aggressive attitude towards the opponents in possession, forcing them to play in difficult conditions and along horizontal lines, all vertical lines of maneuver having been closed off.
Pressing is therefore an important instrument in regaining possession, but it must be used in a rational and well-organized way because physically speaking it takes a lot out of the players.
Also, because of the position the players must take up on the field (tight marking and anticipation on the supporting players) it does not allow for the creation of adequate covering lines with respect to the ball.
For these reasons a team that is to utilize pressing must be in excellent athletic condition, must be good at moving itself and shortening up on the ball with the right tempo, aware that any delay or bad placement during these defensive moves could facilitate a dumping pass by the opponent leading to a favorable situation of play for our adversaries. As we have already pointed out, whether or not there is pressure on the ball is one of the fundamental keys to the judging of the situation of play in the defense phase. In the end it all comes down to this : is the ball 'covered' or 'uncovered'?
The principle I am trying to get at is the following: aggressive defending on opponents in possession by the players in their zone sets up a situation allowing the whole team to have an assertive attitude when they are marking other elements of the opposing team.
Apart from putting pressure on the player in possession, the carrying out of good pressing actions also leads to numerical superi-

ority around the ball, with double teaming on the opposing player in possession, tight anticipatory marking of his nearby team mates and preparatory 'T-type' marking on any long passes that he might make to his more distant team mates.
Situations of play that can lead to pressing actions are the following:

❏ the player in possession has his back to our goal;
❏ his pass is too high or off the mark;
❏ on a badly made trap;
❏ on a back pass.
❏ the player hogs the ball or lacks decision.

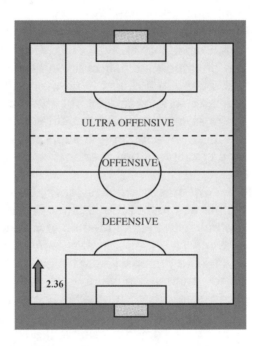

We can distinguish pressing in the following ways, depending on the part of the field in which it is carried out (Fig. 2.36)

- ultra-offensive pressing;
- offensive pressing;
- defensive pressing.

You will choose the type of pressing to carry out by keeping in mind the characteristics of your own team, as well as that of the opposition.

With ultra-offensive pressing you have decided to attack your opponents in great depth, aiming to make sure that their defense is not free to build up play. The advantage of this type of pressing is that once we have regained possession our players are near the opponent's goal and in a good position to try to score. The defense will have to play very far into depth and will be using off-side tactics all the time so that they can dominate the large amount of ground behind them. You will need these kinds of strikers: physically strong, not too fast and good in the air. This type of pressing is normally used against teams that we consider weak, even though it can also be applied against stronger teams in order to keep them as far as possible from our goal.

Offensive pressing is carried out in the opponent's half, and, because we will now have more space to cover during our counter-attacking moves than with ultra-offensive pressing, the team should adapt itself to exploiting this range of distances. This type of pressing is usually carried out when balanced teams are playing against each other.

Defensive pressing is carried out in our own half, and it aims to set off the abilities of our strikers, who will be fast and capable of using the wide open spaces in counter-attack. This type of pressing is used by teams that prefer a strategy permitting them to close off spaces in the defense phase, regaining possession by intercepting passes and making fast counter-attacking ploys. You can make this choice when you are facing a stronger team or in cases where your own team is in advantage.

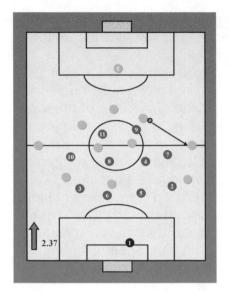

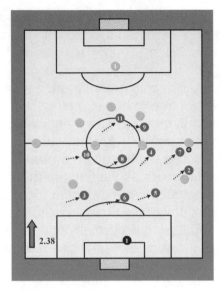

Invited pressing is another thing. This is a defensive attitude and placement of the team which aims to channel the opponent's moves in the direction of a certain player (usually the least gifted technically) or a certain part of the field, and then apply pressing. For example, if our defense strategy calls for pressing along the sidelines, the team will tighten up when the ball is in the central area, closing off the spaces there so as to 'invite' the opponents to develop their plays along the sidelines where we wish to attack them (Fig 2.37 and 2.38).

OFFSIDE

Offside tactics are an important means of regaining possession. They can be divided into active and passive ploys.
In the first case, the opponent is put into an offside position by an up field movement of the defense section. In the second situation the offside is created by the movement of a striker who goes beyond a defense line that is not moving into depth (an important thing in these cases is the defender's 'follow and quit' movement in the zone of a striker who is just going beyond the line).
Active offside tactics are collective defense actions which must be used with intelligence and care especially in the amateur youth sector, where the absence of linesmen makes it difficult for the referee to evaluate the offside rule with any accuracy.

The problem is that, if carried out badly, the active use of offside tactics will hand the opposing team a very good chance to score because one of their players will find himself face to face with the goalkeeper.

This paragraph should be read keeping firmly in mind what has already been said regarding the vertical movements of the defense.

In fact, we have already defined the playing situations that can lead to the application of offside tactics when we were looking at the in-depth movements of the defense line.

Pressure on the ball is the indispensable condition ensuring the effectiveness of this defensive action.

Going into depth with the defense to apply offside on an uncovered ball can be extremely dangerous for our team, because at that point the opponent in possession will be free to choose the best play to make without being attacked by the defenders who are moving up and cannot cover each other.

For this reason, the defense line must be able to make correct and unified judgments about covered and uncovered balls, moving up and back in consequence and being ready as well to manage any opposing mid fielders breaking into play.

The goalkeeper has an important role in carrying out offside tactics. As the defense is moving into depth he must take up the correct position out of the goal in order to act as an extra sweeper.

It is vitally important that the coach establishes the strategy governing his team's use of this tactical ploy, paying particular attention to the zone on the field from which it will be put into effect.

If we have decided to use in-depth offside - i.e., near the mid field line - the defense will continue to move up as long as the ball is covered.

On the other hand, active offside tactics can be considered as a natural consequence of the defense's movement to shorten up on the ball in order to keep the right distance from the mid field. In that case, after we have made a long pass from the back, for example, or when our opponents have made a back pass, the defense section will move up to a pre-established depth (I would advise the three-quarter zone), and will go no further, even if the ball is covered.

PROGRESSIVE EXERCISES IN TEACHING THE DEFENSE PHASE

We will now illustrate a graded itinerary for training the defense phase. We will be considering progressive coaching (from exercises in connection with the simplest situations on to more complicated circumstances), paying particular attention to the positive and negative transition phase (the best choices to make and the immediate build up of the counterattack on the one hand, rapid and forceful defensive repositioning on the other). All this will be in line with what we have being trying to illustrate: our idea of the organization necessary to make sure that the phase of non-possession will be **ACTIVE** and **RESOURCEFUL**.
The following exercises are only a few of the many it would be possible to describe, and in any case they should only be taken as a jumping off point for the creation and the carrying out of others more fitting to the needs of your team.

EXERCISES 17, 18 AND 19

The 1 against 1
It is vital to train players in the one against one. It goes without saying that if our players prevail in man to man play , they are sure to win the match. You have to train the 1 vs. 1 in all its aspects, by which I mean:

❐   with the defender facing the player in possession;
❐   with the defender sideways to the player in possession;
❐   with the defender behind the player in possession whose back is turned (Fig 2.41)

EXERCISE 17

Face on 1 against 1
Two players face each other in a 15 x 10 yd. rectangle with two small goals placed at each base line but not directly in front of each other (Fig. 2.39).
The defender has to shorten up as tightly as he can on the striker, trying to slow him down, playing for time and accompanying

him if the player in possession has full control of the ball.
An important thing here is the position of the feet: the defender
must attack his opponent from the side (never frontally) with his
inside foot in front of the other, which will be in line with the direction the ball is moving in.
A defending player must have an active attitude, trying to force
the striker to whichever zone he thinks best (for the most part
onto the sidelines), keeping his eyes fixed on the ball so that he
will not be taken in by the opponent's dummies and dummying
his own tackle so as to put the attacking player in difficulty. Lastly,
the defender must choose the best moment for his intervention,

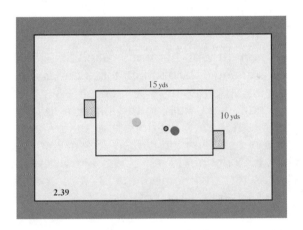

EXERCISE 18

1 + goalkeeper against 1 from the side
In one half of the field a striker in possession will - on being given
the signal by the coach - run for the goal and take a shot. At the
same time he will be marked by a defender placed sideways (Fig.
2.40).
The defending player must be good at getting his opponent out of
the center, making sure that he shoots from an angled position.

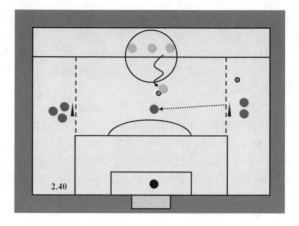

EXERCISE 19

1 against 1, opponent with his back turned.
In a 20 x 15 yd. rectangle divided into three parts, a defender
marks an opponent who has his back turned, with two supporting
players, one on each side, helping the striker (Fig. 2.41). The
defender's job is to not allow his opponent to turn around, and he
must do this without sticking too closely to him but at an arm's
distance so that his opponent cannot use him as a hinge. The
defender will intervene the moment the player in possession is
not covering and defending the ball.

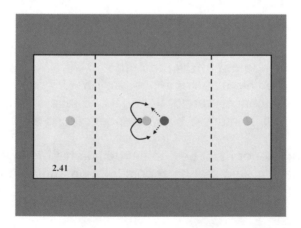

EXERCISE 20

1 + goalkeeper against 2

In one half of the field, a defender faces two strikers who are making for the goal (Fig. 2.42).

This is, of course, a disadvantageous situation for the defender, who will have to place himself at a midway point between the two strikers, 'dancing' between them. In this case, what you need to do is play for time, with the clear intention of giving your team mates time to recreate numerical equality at least. Here the defender must not let himself be singled out by the opponent in possession, who, by heading directly for him, will be able to make an easy pass to the other player; instead he must be able to judge the situation, working on intercepting the pass when it comes or tackling the striker the moment he gets the chance. If he is unable to regain possession, he should try to make sure that the opposing striker actually shoots at goal from a bad position (from the side or with his weaker foot). A useful weapon for the defender is the offside position, to be used in connection with the possessor's team mate going beyond the line of the ball. In this case, the defender should move up and attack the player in possession. When he has regained possession, he should kick the ball into one of the two smaller goals placed on the halfway line.

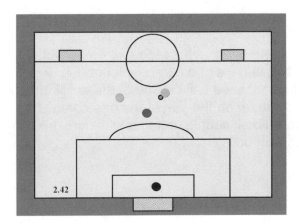

2.42

EXERCISE 21

1 + defender moving back + goalkeeper vs. 2

This exercise is similar to the last, only this time you add a defender placed 30 yards from the two strikers (Fig 2.43).

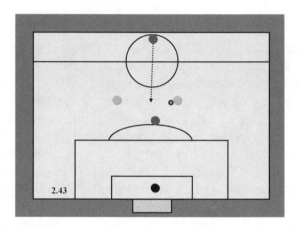

In this case the defender will even more clearly need to play for time. His aim, in fact, is to give his team mate time to move backwards and recreate a situation of numerical equality (2 against 2). When they have regained possession the two defenders must bring the ball across the half way line while being contrasted by the other two.

2 against 1

In a 20 yd square two players face each other with the help of four supporting players in different colours (Fig. 2.44). At a certain point the coach will call on one of these colours, and it will be his job to double up on the player in possession. This exercise helps you to train all double teaming situations (moving up, moving back, section drills).

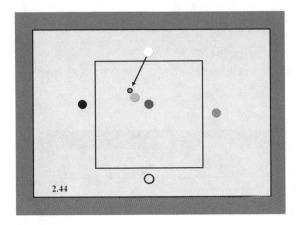

2.44

EXERCISE 23

2 against 2

Two players are facing two opponents in a 20 x 30 yd rectangle, each aiming to bring the ball over the line in front of them (Fig. 2.45).

The 2 against 2 can be considered the basic drill for learning how to move and how to time your marking and your coverage. In this situation the defender does not only link himself in with the strikers, the ball and the goal, but he must also collaborate with a team mate. Here we are beginning to introduce the idea of pressure (and as a consequence of this the other player will put himself in coverage) and pressing (tight anticipatory marking of the supporting player by a team mate) into the defense phase.

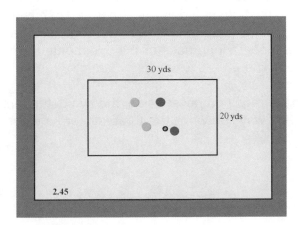

2.45

EXERCISE 24

2 + goalkeeper against 3

Three strikers are facing two defenders in one half of the field (Fig. 2.46).

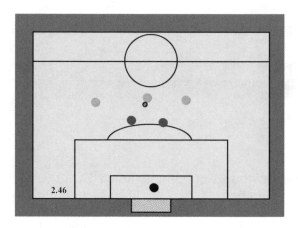

2.46

During a central attack the defenders have to play for time in order to slow down their opponents' play. During a side attack the player in the zone attacks the ball and the other places himself in a covering position half way between the other two opponents; either that or, in cases where there is good pressure on the ball or in situations in which the player in possession is in difficulty, this second defender will go in tight marking on the nearby supporting player, releasing the opponent furthest from the ball. Even in 2 against 3 situations the defenders can utilize offside tactics - when the opponents pass backwards for example, when the defense have made a long pass or the opponents have gone beyond the ball line.

Once they have regained possession, the two defenders have to go over the half way line while the three strikers are contrasting them.

EXERCISE 25

3 against 3

This exercise is similar to N° 14.

In a field measuring 30 x 40 yds, we are playing 3 against 3 aiming to get over the line behind our opponents (Fig. 2.47). Pay special attention to the pressure on the ball, pressing, double teaming, covering and the tight marking of the supporting players near the player with the ball.

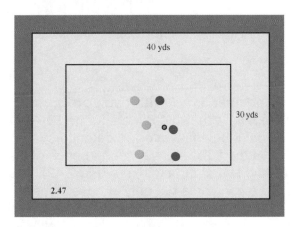

2.47

EXERCISE 26

4 + goalkeeper against 4

In one half of the field four defenders are facing four attacking players (Fig. 2.48).

We are looking at three things in this defense exercise: the concept of 'marking and covering' outside the area; tight marking of the opponents nearby or inside the area; and all vertical or horizontal movements, with particular attention to a unified understanding of covered and uncovered balls. When they have regained possession, the four defenders have to run over the half way line contrasted by the four strikers.

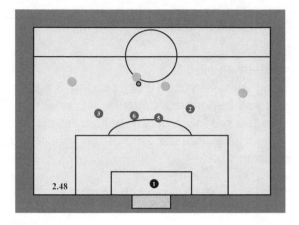

2.48

EXERCISE 27

4 + goalkeeper against 5 or 6 with two corridors.
In one half of the field with two corridors formed by prolonging
the shorter sides of the penalty area, 4 defenders face 5 or 6
strikers lined up in the following way: one in each of the corridors,
one mid fielder and two or three strikers (Fig 2.49). The two players in the corridors can come out only in cases where there has
been a cross from the opposite side. Apart from practicing the
ideas of the last exercise, here you will also be following the side
backs' timing as they shorten in on the opponents placed exter-
nally - as well as the shifts made by the defenders in relation to
the opposing strikers.

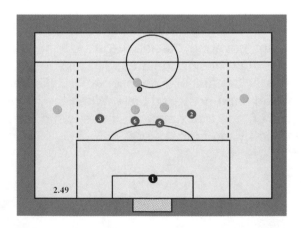

2.49

EXERCISE 28

4 + goalkeeper against 6 or 7.
In one half of the field 4 defenders are facing 6 (4 mid fielders + 2 strikers, 3 + 3) or 7 opponents (4 +3, 5 + 2) (Fig. 2.50). In this exercise, where the defense is in clear numerical inferiority, the determining factor is how well they are respecting the distances between the players and where best to position themselves so as to control the most dangerous opponents (i.e., those nearest to the goal they are defending). An important weapon here will be offside tactics. Once they have regained possession, the four defenders will have to score in one of the three mini-goals placed on the mid field line.

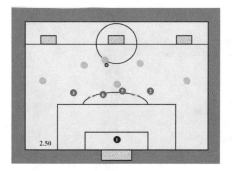 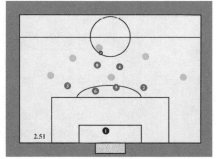

EXERCISE 29

6 + goalkeeper against 6.
4 defenders and 2 center mid fielders are facing 6 opponents (3 + 3, 4 + 2) in one half of the field (Fig. 2.51).

Once they have regained possession, the team defending the goal must get over the half way line.

EXERCISE 30

6 against 7.
Similar to the last exercise, only in this case the four defenders + the two mid fielders are facing 7 opponents (4 + 3, 5 + 2).

EXERCISE 31

8 + goalkeeper against 4 in a passive format
The defense section and the mid field attack the ball brought up by four players placed on the half way line. (Fig 2.52). The mid field carries out the triangle with a central ball and alternates the diagonal with tight marking of the nearby supporting player on external balls. The defense sets up the diagonal on external balls and the line on central play.

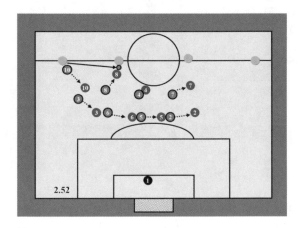

EXERCISE 32

8 + goalkeeper against 6 or 7.
4 defenders face 6 (4 mid fielders + two strikers, 3 + 3) or 7 players (4 + 3, 5 +2) in one half of the field. When they have regained possession they have to get over the mid field line (Fig. 2.53). Due to the situation of numerical superiority, you have to pay special attention here to doubling up on marking

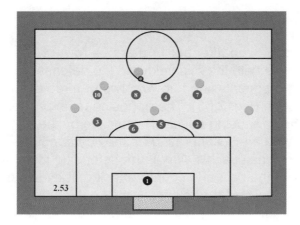

2.53

EXERCISE 33

8 + goalkeeper against 8
As in the last exercise, only in this case the defense and the mid field are facing 8 opponents.

EXERCISE 34

8 + goalkeeper against 11.
The defense and mid field section are facing, first in one half and then on a whole field, a complete team lined up with a particular system (4-4-2, 3-5-2, 3-4-1-2, 4-3-3).

When they have regained possession they must get beyond the half way line (Fig. 2.54).

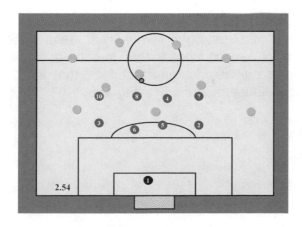

2.54

EXERCISE 35

6 against 6 or 7 + goalkeeper in passive format.

In their offensive half, the mid field and the defense sections are facing 6 or 7 opponents lined up with two or three defenders and four mid fielders. (Fig. 2.55). The opposing team passes the ball around as they are being passively attacked by the mid field and the strikers, who are collaborating as they carry out the defense movements. At the coach's signal, the defending team simulate the recovery of the ball, and counterattack quickly shooting at goal. In the first part of the exercise, they will not be opposed, but then the other team will try to stop them. After they have made a shot, everyone will quickly return to their original positions.

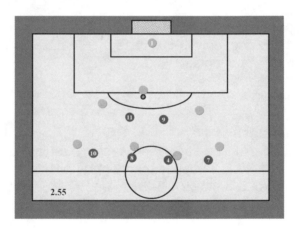

2.55

EXERCISE 36

11 attacking the colors.

First in one half and then on the whole field, a team lined up with the 4-4-2 attacks colored signs placed in parts of the field that the coach considers particularly important. Here they will be carrying out collective defense movements (Fig. 2.56).

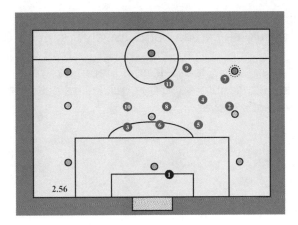

EXERCISE 37

11 attacking various balls.
Following the coach's instructions, a team makes passive attacks on a number of balls placed all around the field as they are carrying out collective defense movements. At the coach's signal, the team involved in the defense simulates ball recovery and counterattacks rapidly shooting at goal. After the shot, pay particular attention to how well and how quickly the team gets back into position.

EXERCISE 38

11 against 5.
On the whole field a team lined up with the 4-4-2 is facing 5 opponents whose aim is to pass the ball 10 times. When they have regained possession the defending team must counterattack and shoot at goal.

EXERCISE 39

11 against 11.
A team lined up in a certain system passes the ball around carrying out various plays (long or short, horizontal or vertical passes, overlapping, breaking in from behind, cuts, crossovers, combinations, dump passes, crosses, etc.). They are faced by a 4-4-2 who carry out their collective movements depending on the build

up and finishing touch techniques put into use by the opponents. The exercise should be carried out passively first of all, and then actively.

In the second case, when the defending team has regained possession they should counterattack as quickly as possible, beating down the opponent's moves.

CHAPTER 3

TEACHING THE ATTACKING PHASE

Andrea Riva

INTRODUCTION

There are a number of basic concepts which every team - and particularly one that is using a zonal system - will have to get a good hold of in order to create an attacking phase that is both composite and truly effective.

In my opinion the group will have to grasp things on a number of different levels, and it is the coach's job to outline a working project that will gradually allow each player to express himself as well as possible in the context of the team.

Though at the beginning more attention will be given to the defense phase, it is vital to come up with precise indications for the attack as well.

In any case it is a good idea to alternate defense plays with exercises teaching the fundamental principles regulating the phase of ball possession, so that, right from the beginning the players get used to carrying out certain movements and will be at an advantage when it comes to facing more specific exercises in offensive tactics.

I will follow the same itinerary, first setting out the basic concepts of the attacking phase and a series of exercises to make sure they are understood, then going on to a more detailed description of the offensive plays connected with the 4-4-2, from the simpler movements of the strikers alone to more complicated ones involving the participation of a greater number of players. I will be having a specific look at plays that foresee the in-line placement of the four mid fielders.

Finally, I will concentrate on how important it is to the dynamics of a team to vary the offensive moves in order to increase the unpredictability of the attack.

THE 4-4-2: BASIC PRINCIPLES

Collective Involvement and the Short Team

A very important thing for a team using the zone is that all its elements should participate in the play.
Connected with this is the team's ability to keep itself compact and short, which means that in the possession phase, the defense line should move into depth (move up in the direction of the opponent's goal), so keeping the correct distance from the mid fielders and favoring a situation of numerical equality.
The defenders must be comfortable receiving the ball and directing play.

EXERCISES

We will be using numbers (3, 5, 11 ...) to indicate players of the team involved in the attacking phase, generally speaking, those more directly involved in the exercise; we will use letters (three, five, eleven ...) for the numbers of players on the opposing team or for those who are not directly implicated in the exercise.

In one half of the field two teams face each other with the only aim of keeping possession. When one team is organizing play, the various members must move around placing themselves so that they can receive a pass while the opponents try to steal the ball by anticipating without directly tackling. When the other team has regained possession you will start over.
Use two, and then one touch play.
At the start the teams will be in numerical equality (from 7 against 7 to 10 against 10), and then with a difference of 1, 2 and finally 3. One team is being trained in how to keep possession when they are in numerical superiority, the other in how to manage the ball even if they are in numerical inferiority.

In a 25 x 25 yd square there are 12 players divided into three teams, each with four players (red, green and blue). All players pass the ball around, then, when the coach gives the signal, if a blue player is in possession the reds and the greens have to take back the ball.

This exercise makes sure players are used to organizing ball possession in situations where the opponents are pressing.

Match in one half of the field, 7 + G (goalkeeper) against 7 + G. Both teams face each other freely, but a goal is good only if all the components of the team have touched the ball at least once during the play. We are aiming for total player participation.

In one half of the field 6 A (attacking players) are up against 6 D (defenders) + G. The attacking players have to score a goal. When the defenders have regained possession, they must, with a minimum of 5 passes, get beyond a line placed 35 - 40 yds from their goal. Here you are coaching positive transition and you are getting the defenders used to playing the ball.

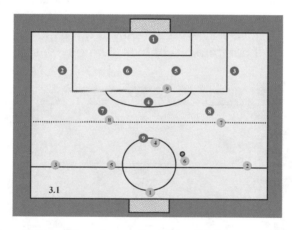

Fig. 3.1. Two teams (8 + G against 8 + G) face each other in one half, then extending to two halves of the field. Their aim is to score, but the goal will only be considered valid if at the moment of the shot all the members of the attacking team are over the dotted line. The defending team will not be too aggressive; they will occupy the spaces, and will begin more determined pressing only when the ball is past the dotted line. The defenders have to move into depth with their team mates, keeping the team short.

Fig 3.2. 8 A against 5 D in one half of the field. The attacking players have to score in one of the two mini goals A and B, passing the ball around the defense. Play begins with 6. For example - he plays to 2, who gives the ball in depth to 7. On a level with the dotted line, 7, with three pressing on him, will play it back to 2 and then the ball has to circulate quickly in defense from 2 to 6 to 5 to 3, if necessary calling on 4 for a dump and rebound pass. Players about to receive the ball must move backwards slightly to gain space. 3 passes to 10 and 8 moves in without the ball ready to take a pass. There is now a two against one situation on the left flank. 10 and 8 have to get past two players and score. Then we begin again from 5, play develops on the left up to the dotted line and then circulates round once more until we get numerical superiority on the right flank. The opposing mid fielder four presses the center mid fielders while the two rival strikers nine and eleven press the center defenders, passively first of all, and then in a more aggressive way. The defenders get used to playing the ball and moving it out from the center towards the sidelines.

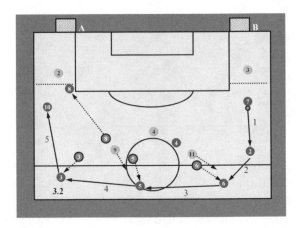

It is very important that the players should follow the flow of the action when the ball is moving from one flank to another. For example, during the play presented in the diagram, at a certain point 6 sends the ball in the direction of the other center defender; having passed the ball, it is a good idea for 6 to move diagonally in the direction of his team mate to give him support. Only when a player decides to change the flank should the side defender furthest from the ball widen out in order to be able to utilize the whole width of the field.

POSITIVE TRANSITION

The moment when we lose or regain possession are very important in the match. It is vital for the team to react well in such situations. Something should galvanize in every player immediately when possession is recovered - we should be able to see a total change of attitude, the whole team must take off.
What we are talking about is a change in mentality. The players must become more resourceful and more effective in their movements, without overbalancing the tactical set up. Goals are very often scored today as a result of rapid counterattacks created by pressing that allows for recovery of possession. There can also be individual counterattacks, sometimes lethal for the opposing defense if the player who has regained possession is able to accelerate with the ball at his feet - though he must be accompanied by his team mates. In any case, it is important to train this phase of play. Even psychologically speaking, the entire team must feel united and react as a block.

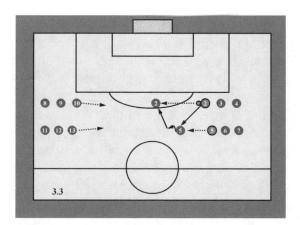

EXERCISES

Fig. 3.3. Here we are not training the group's reaction as much as the anticipation and the continuity of the counterattack carried out by the player who regains possession and a team mate.
Place the players in four lines. 2 and 5 set off, passing the ball back and forth every so often. When they have completed about half the distance, 10 and 13 come out , and they have to choose the right moment to intercept one of the balls passed between

the first two. Whichever of the two recover possession will then make a dash of about ten yards or so, ball at his feet. His team mate will come alongside and they will begin to pass the ball until 3 and 6 come out, regaining possession by intercepting one of their passes. What is important here is how the two players change speed when they recover possession.

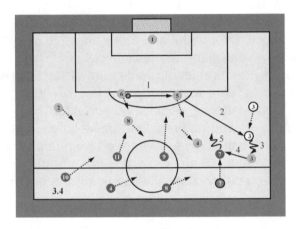

Fig. 3.4. Two teams, 6 A against 6 D + G, are lined up in one half of the field. The opposing backs pass the ball around in defense, and a center defender, for example five, plays wide onto the side-lines towards three who is moving into depth. The whole team of opponents moves up while the others go back towards the mid field, occupying the spaces but not putting up any real resistance. On the mid field line, however, their marking gets tighter, and three makes a pass towards four that can easily be intercepted. 7 intervenes in anticipation, and from this instant the team that has regained possession has from five to seven seconds to conclude the play by taking a shot at goal. It is important that you can see a change of pace in all the players during the transition; the strik-ers must put the ball into depth, the center mid fielders must fol-low play and give support, the side player on the weak side (the side of the field where the ball is not in play in contrast to the strong side) must tighten in towards the ball to give coverage. Depending on the opponent's set up, we can decide to counterat-tack with the ball at our feet or dump it on a team mate, but in any case we must follow the action. The opponents who have lost the ball will put up passive resistance first of all, then become more aggressive.

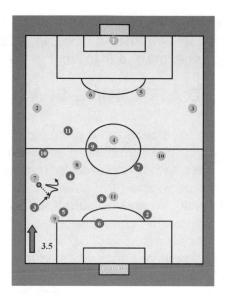

Fig. 3.5. The situation is 10 A against 10 D + G on a whole field. The opposing team (with the goalkeeper) passes the ball around, alternating side changes and short and in-depth passes. The team in the defense phase positions itself as a consequence, depending on the position of the ball, carrying out diagonals and horizontal shifting movements without really trying to regain possession. When the coach gives the signal, the player receiving the ball must stop for about two seconds; the defending team are not to contrast him, but place themselves in such a way as to intervene in anticipation of his next pass. After two seconds the player will pass the ball to a nearby team mate, and, if the movements have been rapid and organized, the transition will come about.

At this point everyone on the team that has regained possession will sprint a yard or two into an offensive forward move; the defense line will come to a halt while play proceeds quickly until a shot at goal. You can decide whether or not the team that has lost possession should go into the defensive phase.

Apart from training positive - and possibly also negative - transition, this is a useful exercise because it gets the players used to carrying out invited pressing, i.e., to make sure that they know how to line themselves up to intercept a pass from an opponent under pressing or who is in difficulty. Also, because it is the coach's signal that sets off pressing, you can get counterattacks from the attacking zone, the mid field zone or the defensive zone.

CREATING AND ATTACKING SPACE

A team's attacking play is based to a great extent on the concepts of creating and attacking space. The players must widen out and lengthen the opposing defense by making movements without the ball; in other words they have to force them to cover a greater area of the field, so making sure that the defenders do not find themselves in numerical superiority or at least creating such problems for them.

Going in to occupy an empty space means forcing the opponents to move in order to carry out marking. In the same way, by concentrating a lot of players in a restricted area on the field, we will make their job much easier.

It is a good idea to concentrate your attention on the correct timing of play so that the attacking action becomes that much more effective.

EXERCISES

Fig. 3.6. This is a very important exercise aiming to make sure that a player frees himself of his marker before receiving a pass from a team mate. The attacking player creates space in which to receive the ball by returning to a zone that he had abandoned with a dummy movement. The players are placed in groups of four as in the diagram: 4 and 8 are passing the ball to each other, and, at the coach's signal, the player who receives the ball must send it into depth towards 9, who, at the moment of the signal, will have sprinted forward followed by his defender. Suddenly 9 will change direction, moving back and gaining a yard or two on his direct marker. He will now be able to receive his team mate's pass undisturbed and carry out a rebound pass. 8 receives the rebound from 9 and either shoots or restarts the original series of passes, dumping on 4. This is a useful exercise for training playing tempo as well: 9 must not make his move too early, otherwise the defender will have time to tighten up the marking before the pass arrives to its destination; on the contrary, if he starts late he will not be able to create the necessary space.

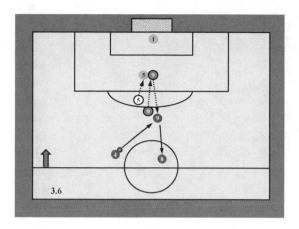

3.6

Fig. 3.7. 4 A against G. 4 and 8 pass the ball around. 9 and 11 keep in constant movement. At the coach's signal 4 calls to 9 and dumps the ball on him. Coming forward to meet the ball, 9 passes first time to 8, who immediately sends it vertically in the direction of 11, who has come diagonally the take up the space left free by 9. 11 makes a one touch shot at goal. You can do this first of all without defenders as in the diagram, then add one or two markers.

The illustration shows the classical movement of the strikers - one to meet and one into depth. Here as well, the players will have to be careful that they are passing with the right timing. It would be no good, for example, if 11 arrived into position before 8 made the pass because the opponents would have the time to reposition themselves and effectively defend the shot. In this light, the diagram gives two options for 11's movements without the ball: he can play for time after 9 has moved away and then cut in; or, as 9 is moving, he can go wide towards the left, only to change direction at the right moment and carry out his cutting movement. In this exercise, the coach's signal is an important point of reference as far as the timing of the play is concerned, but it is a good idea to repeat the set up leaving the decision of when actually to carry out the in-depth pass to the discretion of the mid fielder. In this case, 9 will have to be watching his team mate in order to catch the exact moment when he should start his movement.

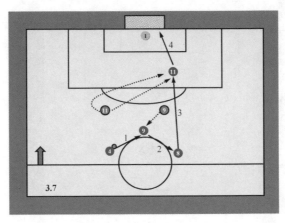

Fig. 3.8. 4 A against G. Attacking space with diagonal cuts from the offensive apex while the second striker moves into the space created by the team mate and gives him an in-depth ball.

9 has his back to the opposing goal. 11, 7 and 4 are watching him. Suddenly 9 turns round and sprints off diagonally towards one of the two cones behind him. If he makes a move towards cone B, as in the figure, 7 goes in diagonally to take up the place vacated by 9 (if 9 makes for cone A, 11 will be the one to go towards the center). 4 makes a vertical pass to 7; controlling the ball, 7 will then bring it to the left beyond cone A, passing it verti- cally to 9, who has in the meantime made a change of direction towards the left beyond cone A. 9 immediately shoots at goal.

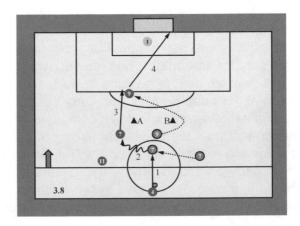

SUPPORTING AND DEPTH

In today's soccer, speed is of the essence, which leads to a reduction in the time players have to carry out their plays. As a consequence it is a good thing for players to be facing the goal when carrying out a pass. This will give them a better vision of play and will save them time in ball control. What we need then is to effect a series of passes backwards and forwards. In this context, the movements of the supporting players become important (a player presents himself for a possible backward pass from his team mate in possession). Other players must also move into depth to gain field.

EXERCISES

Fig. 3.9. A match in one half of the field, 9 + G against 9 + G. We want two touch play, and the defending team is not aggressive - it allows the other team to play and only regains possession by anticipation. The attacking team is to alternate between passing back and passing forward.
We can see an example in the diagram: 6 is in possession; 8 comes up to him and receives the pass; after passing, 6 has to decide whether to support play or keep his position. In this case, 2 is supporting play and so 6 plays for time, ready to move into depth so as to keep the team short when there is an in-depth pass.. 8 dumps on two, and this back pass must be as precise as possible; 2 then makes a one touch return pass into depth, accommodating 7's movement. 7 controls the ball and looks for a supporting player behind him, presumably 8, who can give to 9, and so on.
Players passing forward should not go into depth, in order not to unbalance the team, though it goes without saying that for every backward pass there should be an in-depth movement on a team mate's part.

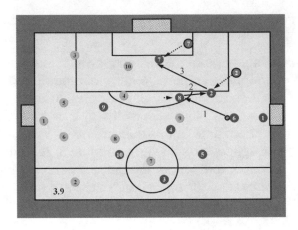

Fig. 3.10. On the whole field, 10 A against G. Play begins from the center defender (5 in the diagram), and he widens out to 3; coming to meet him, 11 receives the pass and dumps on 4, who passes immediately to 9; another dump on 8 who passes wide on 7's movement into depth. 7 moves up with the ball and crosses to the center where 10 and 11 cross over trying to shoot. Repeat this play starting from the right side.

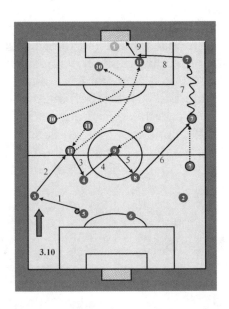

THE TOWER, AND ATTACKING FROM THE SIDELINES

Two very frequently used plays, which we will be having another look at when describing the offensive plays peculiar to the 4-4-2, are connected with the use of the tower. Here we are talking about high dump and rebound passes on a central striker good with his head, and how to use the sidelines. This last is a fundamental aspect of play because one of our fundamental principles is that it is necessary to use the whole width of the field during the offensive phase to stretch out the opponent's defense.

EXERCISES

Fig. 3.11. Two teams are facing each other 11 against 11 in the part of the field between the two areas.
As shown in the diagram, two rectangles 4 - 5 yards wide and of the same length as the penalty area are lined out at about 10 or 11 yards from the two goals. Inside these two rectangles is an area A. Only two attacking players on the team in possession can take turns entering this rectangle - but they can never do so at the same time. The opposing defenders can mark them, but they are not allowed to enter area A. The aim is to score a goal, and the only rule is that goals will be valid only if the pass preceding the shot was carried out by one of the two strikers, who must be inside the rectangle and are only allowed to touch the ball twice (or once if they do so with their head). In the example, player number 10 dumps on 9 who is inside the rectangle; 9 rebounds backwards onto 4 who has a shot on goal. This exercise can also be done with a single attacking player

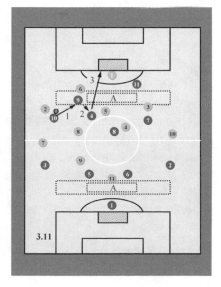

3.11

staying fixed in area A, but in the version that we have presented we are expecting more mobility - even on the sides - from our two center forwards, and we want them above all to be watching each other so they do not find themselves in the rectangle at the same time. Also, we are getting them accustomed to playing at staggered levels and not on the same line.

Fig. 3.12. On a small-sized field, 10 against 10. Three touch play at most. The two teams face each other with the aim of scoring in the mini-goals located on the base line away from the center (see diagram). What we are trying to do here is to coach players in switching play and developing their maneuver along the side-lines.

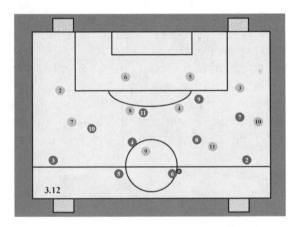

3.12

Fig. 3.13. A reduced field is divided lengthwise into three parts, as in the diagram. Two teams, each composed of six players plus the goalkeeper, face each other in the central area. There is also one player in each external area along the sides. These two play-ers (wild cards) play with whichever team happens to have pos-session. Goals are valid only if they have been created by a cross from one of the side players, and neither team can make more than three consecutive passes in the center zone without widening play to the sidelines.

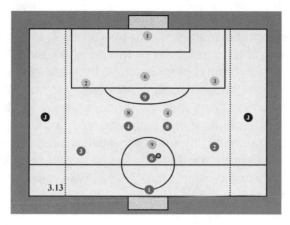

Fig. 3.14. A match 11 against 11 in that part of the field between the two penalty areas. The field is divided lengthwise into three sectors (the dotted lines in the diagram). Goal scoring plays will be accepted only if they have come about as the result of a cross from the sidelines. Both teams can place a man inside each external zone. As soon as there is a direct pass towards an outer sector, another player on the team in the offensive phase can (or must) enter that area, so creating a situation of numerical superiority two against one, which must then be exploited (triangles, overlapping) until you get a cross.

It is a good idea to have the sidelines occupied principally by the side players of the mid field and the defense, or, if necessary, by the center mid fielders. In the diagram the center defender 5 gives the ball to 4, who widens to 10 in the left hand sector. The moment this last pass takes place, the side defender 3 enters the left sector and carries out external overlapping on 10, who gives him the ball to get free of the opposing defender two's opposition. 3 crosses and 11 shoots at goal after having made a crossover with 9.

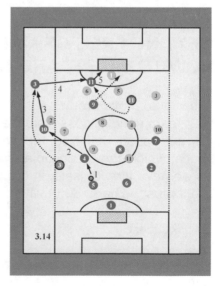

Fig. 3.15. The field is divided as shown in the diagram: a central area C, two external sidelines B and two areas A around the goals. Each team has a defender in the defense area A, a mid fielder in zone C, two players for each of the side areas B and two strikers in the attacking zone A. We thus get numerical superiority in the attacking zone and numerical equality in the mid field (1 against 1 in the middle and 2 against 2 along the sidelines). Goals can only be scored by one of the two strikers receiving a cross from the sidelines. Defenders and side players can exchange balls with the center mid fielder, who must carry out one touch play.

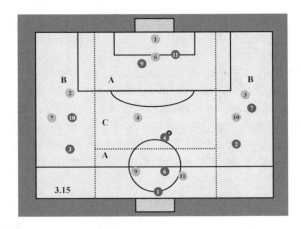

GETTING FREE OF MARKING:
HOW TO TIME IT AND HOW TO DO IT

It is vital to move around without the ball to give extra solutions to your team mate in possession, at the same time creating difficulty for your opponents. Also, a player on the move creates an empty space, which can be occupied by a team mate.
As we have already said, in order for attacking play to be effective it must be carried out with the correct timing.

EXERCISES

Fig. 3.16. 15 cones are placed at random over a part of the field with an area of 35 x 35 yds 5 or 6 players pass each other the ball along the ground making sure that it does not touch the

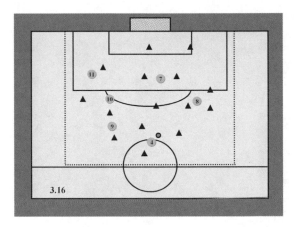

3.16

cones. They are allowed two touches: stop and pass; and they cannot pass the ball back to the player from whom they received it. The team mates have to free themselves of marking and, at the same time, attract the attention of the player in possession. It is a good idea for the players to free themselves of marking the moment their team mate carries out the first touch or immediately after he has controlled the ball.

In the second part of the exercise the timing of these successive movements becomes more precise. These are the new dynamics: ball control (first touch), visual contact with the team mate and then the pass itself (second touch). The team mate should get into movement as soon as visual contact has been established.

Fig. 3.17. This exercise is to train the players how to time their attempt to free themselves of marking. Groups of five: as in the diagram, 10, 4 and 8 have their backs to 9 and 11 and are passing the ball around to each other. 11 and 9 are watching them, waiting for one to turn. Suddenly one of the mid fielders (n° 8 in the figure) receives the ball, turns and makes visual contact with one of the two strikers (11 in the figure), who cuts into depth in that very moment and receives the pass.

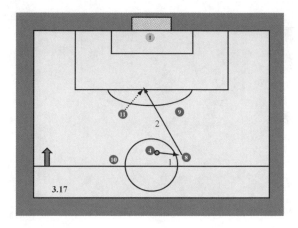

Fig. 3.18. Groups of five, 4 A and 1 D placed as in the diagram. All players are facing 6, who is in possession; he passes to 4, who has a cone behind him as a point of reference. Just as the ball is about to arrive to 4, the opposing defense player (n° four in the figure) brings himself up to the player and can decide whether to go to his right or to his left. In the example he has decided to go to his right; 4 controls the ball and turns immediately, and, noticing that the defender is arriving to his left, looks for a team mate on his right. Visual contact having been made, 9 begins a diagonal backward movement, receives the ball and at once sends it vertically in the direction of 11, who, in the meantime, has attacked the space left free by 9. Note that the movements of the players without the ball should be carried out in different directions - it would be a mistake, for instance, if 9 and 11 were to converge.

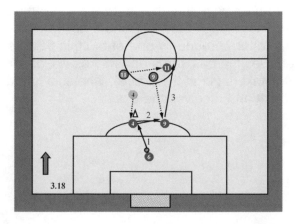

Fig. 3.19. 4 A against G in one half of the field. The set up is as in the diagram: 4 has possession along the mid field line; he brings it between two cones and must then decide whether to go to the right or to the left. In the example he goes towards 10. At this point the team mates begin their movements; 10 must move away in order to create space for 4 who is bringing the ball towards the left flank, and so he cuts in diagonally towards the center, where he finds 9, who has to move in turn (so as not to block up 10's space), and he sets himself up for the pass by making an external cut; 7 moves up parallel to 10, but when he notices that 10 is moving in the same direction, decides to cross over and go to receive a possible cross level with the near post. In fact, 4 plays into depth on 9, who moving up and around a cone crosses to the center, where 7 and 10 are arriving - and one of these will shoot at goal.

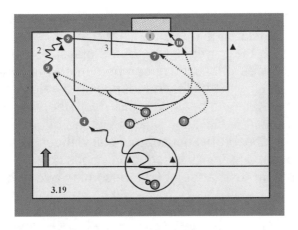

THE 4-4-2 SYSTEM: ATTACKING PLAYS

The 4-4-2 is a playing system that spaces out counterattacks in the best possible way during the defensive phase and whose phase of ball possession can be interpreted more or less offensively, depending on how many players participate in the attack or on how many of them are pessimistically oriented (this is the definition of those players carrying out movements that allow them to intervene promptly in cases where the team loses possession).

Another criteria for establishing a team's grade of offensiveness is to work out exactly how far back the strikers and the side mid fielders should move during the defense phase.

In any case, basing himself on his own ideas, it is up to the coach to find the right tactical balance which will allow the team to be dangerous in front and not find itself off-balance during negative transition.

One of the cardinal principles of the defense phase - getting numerical superiority near the ball - clearly acquires extra weight during the possession phase. For that reason, we create the so-called chains: groups of players that cooperate in the same part of the field, carrying out coordinated movements with or without the ball. To that end it is important that in the 4-4-2 the side defenders should participate in the offensive phase.

In any case, the driving force of the attack can only be the two strikers, who, by carrying out their movements will often be governing the development of play.

It is important to follow a precise didactic itinerary so that the players can assimilate the movements and are able to carry them out with regard to the correct timing of the plays. You should begin with exercises whose plays can be carried out very slowly, maybe even passing the ball by hand, paying careful attention to when each player should begin to move. Only then is it alright to gradually increase the difficulty: kicking instead of using hands, stepping up the speed of execution but still without opposition from the defense, and finally introducing opposing players who will put up passive resistance at first, becoming ever more aggressive.

THE MOVEMENTS OF THE TWO STRIKERS

There are a number of offensive plays that involve the two strikers: some of these solutions will be preferred and others disregarded depending on the physical characteristics of the actual players we have on the team and on the type of defense we are facing. In any case, it is always a good idea to vary offensive plays, so as to make sure that our opponents cannot find the right countermeasures to stop our actions.

The pair of attacking players is very often formed by a first striker (tower or apex) who will be physically powerful and good in the air and at rebounding passes, and a second striker who is quick, good at dribbling and able to carry out a wide range of different movements. What they will need to have in common is a good feeling for goals and the ability to give depth to play.

Of course, you will be able to put together strong attacking pairs who do not respond to the requisites we have just laid out. The presence of two towers on the field, for example, will make the team very dangerous on high balls and will give good goal scoring averages from set plays - but it will also force the mid fielders to be heavily engaged in offensive movements.

Two quick strikers make it easier to counterattack; they create difficulties for slow defense systems; and, being good at dribbling, will also come in very handy against man marking defenses, in that, with situations like this, you are likely to get several direct 1 against 1 face-offs. The disadvantage is that you will not have the assistance - often fundamental for a team in difficulty - of a first striker able to protect the ball and to allow the mid fielders and the defenders to move up behind.

In the following pages I will be setting out the movements typical of the offensive plays connected with the two strikers of the 4-4-2.

Support and depth

This is a classic movement of the two strikers: one goes to meet the player in possession and the other breaks into the space left free by the first, so giving vital depth to the action..

Looking at Fig. 3.20: if 11 sees that his team mate in possession is relatively free, he can at once decide to attack the space left free by 9 and call for a direct pass into depth. At this point the mid fielder has two alternatives: he can either dump a short pass on 9 or he can go for a long vertical pass to 11. If 4 does not pass to 11, this player must move back so as not to finish up in an offside position.

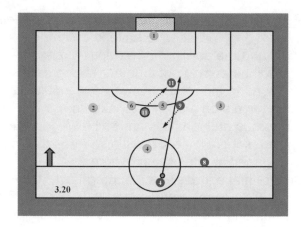

3.20

There is another solution: 11 can decide to play for time after 9 has gone to meet the player in possession, and this is something he should do in particular if he notices that 4 cannot pass into depth because he is being pressed by the opponents. In such cases (Fig. 3.21), 11 carries out an L-shaped movement, i.e., he widens out, ready to cut in diagonally immediately should one of his team mates find himself in a position to pass him the ball. In the figure, 9 receives the ball from 4, he dumps on 8, and just as 8 is about to receive the ball, 11 calls for the in depth pass. 11 can widen out towards the left, as in the diagram, or towards the right to cross over with 9's supporting movement. It is a good idea for 8 to look for depth towards 11, and he should go for other options, usually widening play out towards the sidelines, only when this pass is not possible

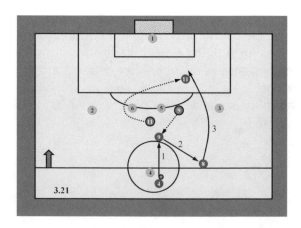

3.21

After having dumped the ball, 9 will give depth going in the opposite direction from the one in which he passed the ball.

This extremely quick and elastic movement of the two strikers has the advantage of widening out the opposing defense, which will, among other things, make it easier for any mid fielders to break into play. In general, however, it will create particular difficulties for defense sections drawn up in line.

The play illustrated in 3.22 is a very useful one, especially if one of the two strikers is good at aerial play.

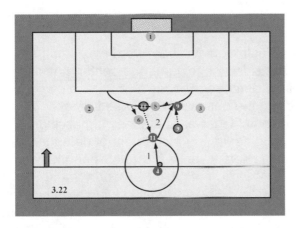

3.22

In the example in the figure, 11 comes to meet the player in possession, and, just as he is about to receive the ball, 9 moves into depth. 11 must be able to make a first touch wall pass towards his team mate. Teams that are using a tower (player 11 in this example) usually make wide use of this play because it is extremely difficult to defend a striker good with his head who 'tips' the ball in the direction of the second striker.

CUTS

We are talking about a similar movement to the last, because, in most cases, a team mate will first need to move away in order to create space. Here, however, this is not a necessary condition; in fact, as we will see later, it can happen that both strikers carry out a cut so as to free space for a mid fielder to break into.

A cut is a diagonal movement into depth to free yourself of marking, which allows you, if you should receive a pass, to protect the ball with your body and shoot at goal.

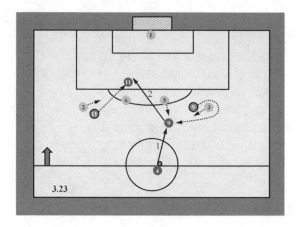

Fig. 3.23 is an illustration of a backward inside cut; i.e., a cut car-ried out from the sidelines towards the center, passing around behind the direct defender: 9 goes to meet the player in posses-sion, n° 4, forcing the opposition defense to move; 11 cuts in diagonally from outside towards the inside, passing behind 6 and anticipating the tightening up movement of defender two. 4 pass-es to 9, who immediately sends it on between the two central defenders in the direction of 11; it is important that 9 gains some space on his direct marker, perhaps playing a dummy and chang-ing direction so as not to give the defenders time to close off the passing lines. If the opposition defense is very tight towards the strong side, 11 can also cut in behind the last defender (n° two in the example).

This is a very useful movement, especially against zonal defense, because it forces the defenders to keep an eye on the ball at the same time they are looking after the attacking player, who is run-ning diagonally starting from the weak side. In addition, when 11 receives the ball he will probably have the defenders two and six on his tail, but he can control with his right foot, placing his body between the ball and his opponents and prepare himself to shoot, again with his right foot (this is a classic movement of the wings in a three man attack, which, for this reason, often foresees the use of a left-footed player as the right side striker or vice versa). Depending on how far he is to the side, 11 must start his cut when 9 receives the ball or just before.

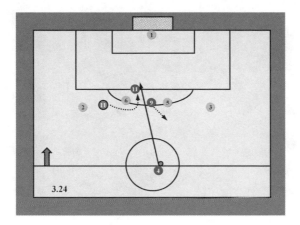

3.24

In figure 3.24 we see an inside cut into depth: 9 tries to bring defender five wide and 11 starts off from behind 6, passing in front of him and cutting in diagonally to receive 4's vertical pass. In this case it is 9 who sets off the play: when 11 sees his team mate widening out he begins the action, trying to surprise defender six; 4 must carry out the pass before 11 is over the defense line. 11 can protect himself from six's intervention by shooting at once or by bringing the ball on with the inside of his right foot.

In Fig. 3.25 we see a ring cut, useful to get round players marking the man. This is a good movement for the second striker because it has to be carried out with great speed. 11 brings defender five away while 9 starts a movement towards the player in possession; suddenly he accelerates and changes direction, creating problems for defender six, who finds himself having to carry out a fairly complicated movement very quickly and without warning. In this way, 9 can gain a yard or two and cut into depth towards the center, receiving the pass from 4.

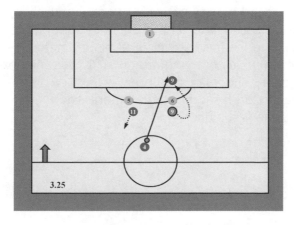

3.25

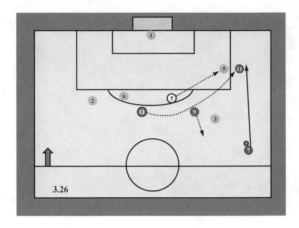

3.26

In Fig. 3.26 we have an outside cutting movement (from the center towards a sideline). This will not lead to a shot on goal, but it often creates 1 against 1 situations along the sidelines. It is usually carried out if the player in possession is decentralized towards one of the sidelines. In the diagram, the right side mid fielder is in possession; the striker nearer to him is giving him support for a short pass, while the other attacks the space left free and cuts diagonally towards the side ready to receive a pass along the sideline from 7. You can invert the roles of the two strikers: the nearest one can create depth and the one furthest away act as support, depending on their distance from the ball.

Dump and rebound

This is very often used by teams that have a tower. As we can see in 3.27, the first striker, 9, dummies going into depth, but then suddenly comes back and takes up position, while, after having widened out (useful not only to achieve the right playing time but also to gain space on the direct opponent) the second striker, 11, cuts to the inside in front of his team mate. 4 dumps towards 9 when he is changing direction; 9 rebounds onto 11's cut, and he either shoots or continues with the action. As an indication, 11 must start his cutting movement when 4 carries out his pass towards the first striker.

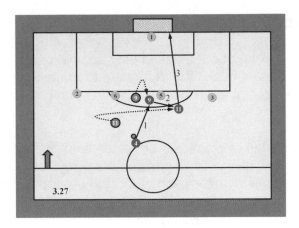

3.27

One - two

This Is effective against in-line defense systems, especially when the two center defenders are not very fast. The example is in Fig. 3. 28. The second striker, 9, is in possession; he brings the ball on, making for a defender (n° five) in an aggressive way. As he comes up to him, the first striker, 11 in the figure, carries out a quick movement in the direction of this team mate. Near defender five, 9 makes a short, crisp pass towards 11, changes pace and overtakes the defender on the right. 11 immediately gives him the ball back, passing it into depth. The first striker can carry out the rebound even if he has his back to the opponent's goal.

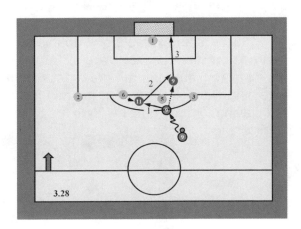

3.28

Crossovers

Here we are talking about a useful play against teams marking the man because it forces the defenders to make intricate movements in the attempt to follow the attacking players they are controlling.

In Fig. 3.29 we see a crossover between strikers 9 and 11, who cut in diagonally, giving 4 two passing opportunities. The two strikers must be fairly near each other and not too far away from the ball.

In Fig. 3.30 we have a crossover as the ball is being crossed: the striker furthest from the ball has to cut to the nearest post while the other moves away in a horizontal direction, then cuts in towards the far post.

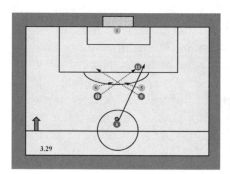 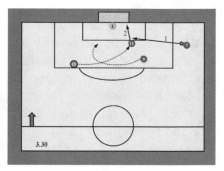

Lastly, in Fig. 3.31 there is an example of a double crossover, which can be carried out if both strikers are extremely fast. Defense systems marking the man run great risks in their attempt to mark this type of movement. However, the mid fielder needs to be very good at playing for time until he finds the right moment to carry out his vertical pass.

Blocking

Borrowed from basketball, this is a very effective play against defense systems marking the man. The basic idea is to place your body between a team mate and the man that is marking him so as to make it difficult for the defender to keep tight control on the attacking player.

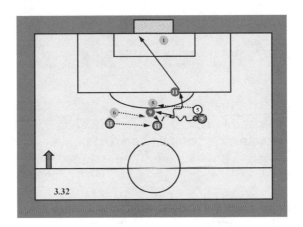

3.32

In Fig. 3.32, 9 is in possession; he is being tightly marked by defender five as he runs in towards the center with the ball, followed by the man controlling him. 11 is being marked by six, and he carries out the opposite movement going right up alongside his team mate, who lets him have the ball. At this point, the opposing defender six will have difficulty following 11 because he will find 9's body in the way in front of him. The defenders will have to be good at exchanging the man they are marking, otherwise 11 will be able to gain space and shoot.

In Fig. 3.33 we have an example of a block in the area, which can be very useful when taking free kicks from the corner. The first striker, 9, makes a passive block in favor of 11, who is passing nearby, escaping in this way from the control of his own marker.

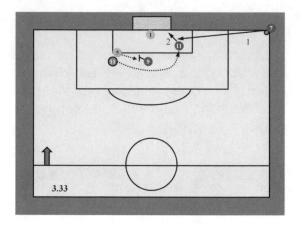

3.33

Veil

This is not a simple movement and requires a lot of intuition between the two strikers, but if it is carried out correctly it guarantees excellent results on account of the degree of unpredictability connected with it.

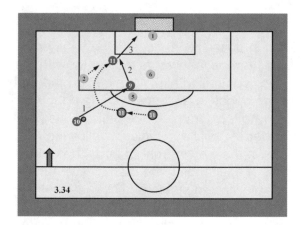

3.34

In Fig. 3.34 the left side mid fielder is in possession. The second striker 11 carries out a movement towards the left; 10 passes towards 9; 11 must find himself on the trajectory of the ball, pretend to intercept it, only to let it go on behind him in the direction of the first striker. After the veil, 11 looks for depth by making an inside cut and receives a one touch pass from 9. The opposing defender, five, surprised by 11's dummy, will not be able to intercept the pass on its way to 9, and he will find it difficult to mark 11.

Heel kick

As with the veil, this is a difficult movement for the rival defense to predict, and can take them by surprise. In this case, however, you must carry out a highly difficult technical move: the running heel kick.
As you can see in Fig. 3.35, striker 9 is calling for an in-depth pass; he receives the ball from mid fielder 8, and plays it behind him with his heel to 11 who is crossing over towards the center and will be able to shoot at goal.

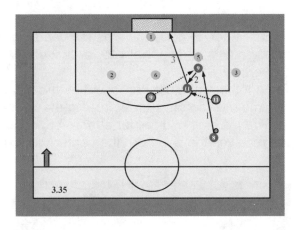

9 cannot look at 11 and so it is 11 that must be good at choosing the right timing for his movement so as to come running up to the point where his section team mate's heel pass will probably be directed.

Cuts to allow the side mid fielders to break in

In carrying out this play it is not our aim to give the ball to the strikers but to use their movements so that the side mid fielders can break dangerously into play in the heart of the opponent's defense.
In Fig. 3.36 we present a double external cut. 9 goes to the right and 11 to the left, so liberating the central part of the attacking front.

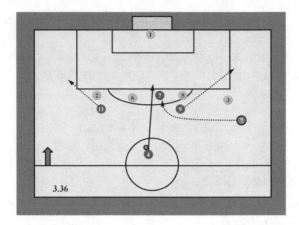

3.36

The right side mid fielder, 7, goes towards the center, crosses over with 9 and then cuts in diagonally towards the area, where he receives 4's vertical pass.

Fig. 3.37 shows another double external cut by the strikers, who both go in the same direction this time, freeing the left part of the attacking area. The left side mid fielder attacks space with an internal cut and receives the ball from the center mid fielder 8.

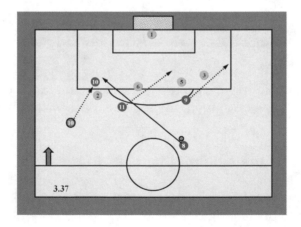

3.37

THE MOVEMENTS OF THE MID FIELDERS

As we have already underlined, it is vital for the coach to create a balanced tactical set up. Considering this, and if you wish to attack with a number of players, it is important to keep the distances between the sections short, telling the defense and the mid field lines to move into depth. When the team has grasped these principles, we can then link up the attacking maneuvers in such a way that more players are involved, thus making play more dangerous and unpredictable.
In the 4-4-2 system assistance supplied by the side mid fielders is particularly important. They can take turns in the attack, or can sometimes even do so at the same time, but only if the center mid fielders remain in coverage and the side defenders converge towards the mid field.
In the following pages we will be describing a number of plays showing the possible developments of linked up attacking maneuvers. There are of course numerous variants that could be added to such plays, and the coach will have to decide himself which will be best for the players he has on hand.

Side mid fielders

In Fig. 3.38, we can see the movements a side mid fielder can make without the ball if a center mid fielder is in possession. The side player can choose one of these depending on the opponents and the movements of the two strikers.

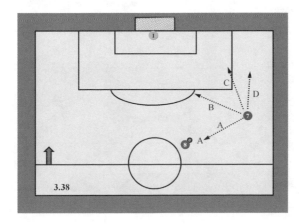

3.38

Movement A is made going to meet the player in possession, so freeing the sidelines and inviting the side defender to an overlap. There is an example of this is Fig. 3.39.

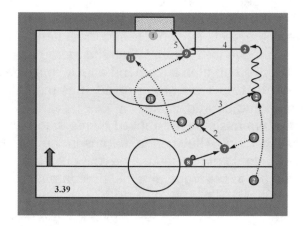

Player 8 is in possession, 7 comes to meet him and 2 carries out external overlapping. At this point play can develop in different ways: in the diagram, 7 receives the ball from 8; he gives it to 11 who has come up in support, and who then widens out towards 2, who crosses. After having completed an L-shaped movement, 9 is now on the near post, while 11 will have gone to the far post after passing to the sidelines.

As an alternative, depending on the opposition's placement on the field, 8 could pass directly to 11 or 2.

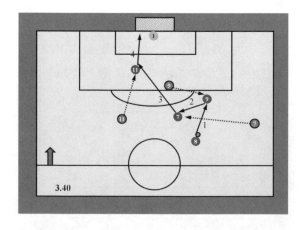

Movement B in Fig. 3.38 indicates an internal cut to receive the ball. This is a very effective movement if you want to receive the ball between the opponent's lines.

There are at least two options for the ensuing development of play: the first is presented in Fig. 3.40, where 7 cuts in and receives 9's rebound from 8's dump. Once 7 is in possession he passes into depth following on the other striker's cut in - this player (n°11) then shoots at goal.

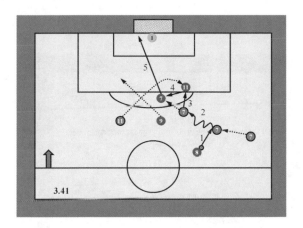

3.41

Alternatively, as in Fig. 3.41, 7 receives the ball directly from 8, brings it on for a few yards and then completes an internal triangle with 11 who has just concluded a sudden change of direction following a crossover with 9. Having received the rebound from 11, 7 can shoot at goal or pass to 9.

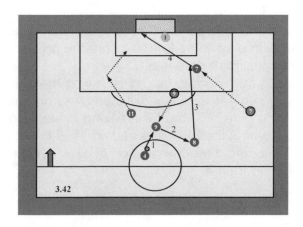

3.42

The movement marked with the letter C in Fig. 3.38 gives depth to the maneuver. Its aim is a shot or a cross under the goal, and it will require the movement of the strikers, who will have to create space to be broken into.

In fig. 3.42, 9 goes in support of 4, receives the ball and dumps on 8, who passes vertically into depth in the direction of 7, who has attacked the space left free by the striker. The mid fielder 7 can now take a shot at goal or pass to 11, who has moved onto the far post.

Lastly, movement D in Fig. 3.38 has two main purposes.

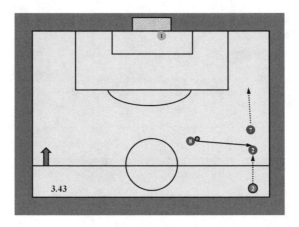

The first, as in Fig. 3.43, is simple but important. Here, we want to give depth to the team on the flanks and allow the side defender to move up. He can receive the ball around the mid field line and set up the play. In the second case, the side mid fielder arrives to the point where he can cross. As shown in Fig. 3.44, it is a good idea for the side player to receive the ball as a result of a sudden change in play so as to make sure the pass is not intercepted by the opposition's defense.

The play develops from right to left, 11 receiving the ball from 8 and then dumping on 4; this player will then carry out the rebound, changing play in favor of 7 breaking in along the flank. 7 will move up towards the base line and cross. 9 has come up onto the near post, and after dumping on 4, 11 will have to position himself on the far post.

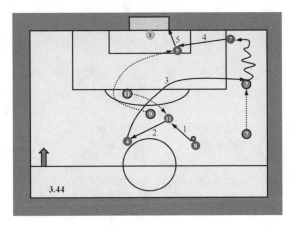

3.44

In Fig 3.45 we can see the possible movements of the side mid fielders in order to receive balls from the side defenders.
Side defenders and mid fielders must be placed in a zigzag formation and not all along the same longitudinal line. This is to make sure that a single defender is not covering several passing lines.

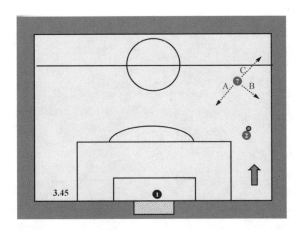

3.45

❐   movement A: the side mid fielder comes in support, freeing the space along the sidelines so that a team mate (center mid fielder or striker) can break in.
❐   movement B: in this case 7 uses the whole width of the field. He places himself on the sidelines so as to receive a pass from 2.
❐   movement C: 7 gives depth to the play, at the same time facilitating the nearest center mid fielder's supporting move away from the center.

When the side mid fielder is in possession, he can carry out a number of possible plays.

DUMPING: the side mid fielder gives the ball to a center mid fielder (horizontal pass, or, even better, a slight diagonal back pass) or backwards towards the side or center defender (but only if there is no risk of being intercepted). He will then carry out the movements described above.

ONE - TWO: you are going for a triangular exchange along the sidelines, getting a dump and rebound from a striker or, more rarely, from a center mid fielder. The triangle can be internal (in order to receive the rebound the mid fielder moves towards the center of the field) or external. Both examples are shown in Fig. 3.46, external triangular passing along the right flank and internal triangular passing along the left flank. The movement is similar to that already described when talking of the strikers. You have to make for your man, dump the ball and then change speed before receiving it again.

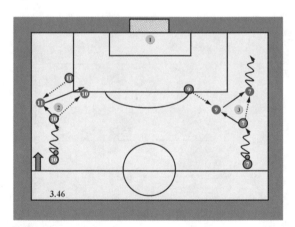

3.46

CHANGING PLAY: this calls for the participation of both side mid fielders and it is a particularly useful movement, especially against defenses that hug tight towards the strong side. As you can see in Fig. 3.47, strikers 9 and 11 carry out movements to free the left side of the attacking front, which will then be occupied by the left side mid fielder, 10, if possible passing behind the last opposing defender. 7 must be able to carry out an accurate long pass across the field to arrive at 10.

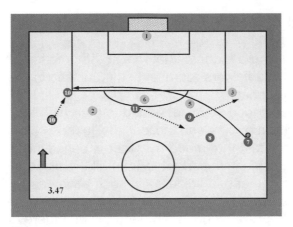

3.47

DRIBBLING: one of the most important abilities of the side mid fielder is beating his man in the one against one. The better he is at that, the more important it becomes to create conditions of numerical equality along the sidelines. In Fig. 3.48, the strikers free the space in front of 7, who is making for the opposing defender three. A dribbling move towards the sidelines is marked A: this is done by moving the ball forward with the outside of the right foot and then - with a sudden change of speed - with the inside of the left. Letter B indicates an abrupt veer towards the center of the field (a right-footed player will hook the ball with the inside of his right foot, a left footed player can use the outside of his left foot, but will find it more difficult to carry out this change of direction, which must be fairly pronounced)

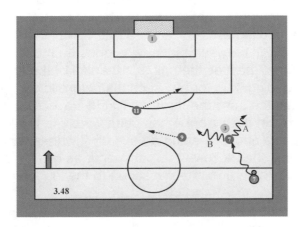

3.48

Center mid fielders

Apart from playing a fundamental role in the defense phase, the pair of center mid fielders represents the nucleus of the team during the build up phase.
They must have good stamina, added to their high technical level, good vision of play and tactical intelligence.
Considering the fact that modern soccer is becoming faster and faster, It is particularly important to train all the players - and especially the center mid fielders - in such a way as to give them the ability to see what is taking place on the field even before they receive the ball. It very often happens that there is simply not time to receive the ball, have a look at how the players are placed on the field, choose the best pass and make it. It is a good idea if you have already decided what to do before you have even received the ball, and so you must keep the ball, your team mates and the opponents constantly under observation.

When he has received the ball, the player will immediately catch the eye of the team mate he has chosen, so calling for his movement; if the players know each other so well that they can find one another with their eyes shut, he can also try a rebound pass. Here is a simple but useful exercise that gets players used to these dynamics: a player (we will call him 7) brings the ball onto the sidelines; a mid fielder (4) follows him from the center, and in front he has another three or four players (9,10 and 11) who are also moving into depth. 7 brings up the ball for a dozen or so yards before meeting a cone - and 15 / 20 yards ahead there is another. While 7 is between these two cones he must pass the ball to 4. Before 7 passes the ball, 9, 10 and 11 take turns putting up an arm, keeping it up for two seconds before lowering it again. When 7 makes the pass the three attacking players no longer have their arms in the air but 4 has been watching the three attacking players and is keeping an eye on 7 who is running with ball on; he must then receive the pass, and, as quickly as possible - without losing precision - pass it on to the last player to put up his arm.
An important task to be carried out by the center mid fielder - but one which is sometimes undervalued - is to receive the ball from his own defenders or the side mid fielders and set up the ensuing

play. Setting up play is a very delicate phase because losing possession in moments like these could be fatal. If the opposition are using in-depth pressing the mid fielders have very little time, and they are also at the disadvantage of having their backs to the opponent's goal.

There are some things we must keep in mind in order to make build up a little smoother: in the first place, as we have already pointed out, it is important to have a good vision of the field even before gaining possession - that will make us aware of whether or not we are being pressed.

A second aspect involves the defenders. They must always be ready as support for a possible back pass from the mid fielder so that they can receive the ball facing the opponent's goal.

Another similar consideration is that it is a good idea for an attacking player to move back to the half way line (how often he can do this will depend on the effectiveness of the opponent's pressing) in order to receive a dump directly from a defender and to rebound on the center mid fielder, who will then be able to control the ball facing the opponent's goal and so set up play more easily.

Lastly, one of the two center mid fielders can move back on a line with the center defenders, and receive the ball from there. In any case, such a movement will free space for the section team mate and for the nearest side defender, to whom the ball could be passed as an alternative.

We will now have a good look at two very useful movements allowing the center mid fielders to free themselves of marking.

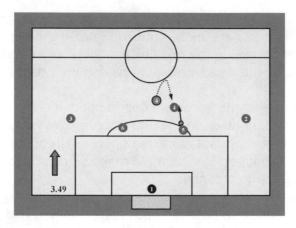

We see in Fig. 3.49 how the center mid fielder, 4, makes a forward movement of a couple of yards, before suddenly halting and
sprinting back. Such a movement allows him to gain space on
the man marking him.

In Fig. 3.50 the right side mid fielder, 7, is in possession. The
center mid fielder nearest to him, 8, makes a movement forwards
and 4, breaks into the space left free and receives the ball.
Generally speaking, when receiving a ball from a team mate, the
mid fielder must take up a position allowing the pass to reach him
in the simplest way, limiting the risk of an interception. Also, if at
all possible, the position he chooses should give him a number of
options for the subsequent pass.
As we can see in Fig. 5.1, a good movement for mid fielder 8,
when 7 is in possession, is to get into a position near but slightly
behind and to one side of 7, so that he can be reached by a diagonal backward pass, which, apart from giving him clear sight of
how to develop play (pass to 11) is also less risky than sending
the ball horizontally (in this case, in fact, if there is an interception, the two players would be completely cut out and there would
be no chance at all of regaining ground).

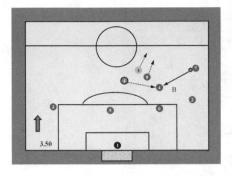 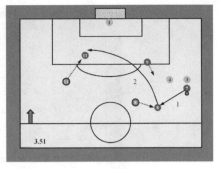

In Fig. 3.52 there is a schematic overview of the possible passing lines:

> A - dump on the center defender;
> B - giving the ball to the side defender who is moving up towards the mid field;
> C - pass to the nearest side mid fielder;
> D - in depth pass along the flank to a side mid fielder or defender;
> E - vertical in-depth pass to a striker;
> F - pass to the supporting striker;
> G - change of play over to the far side;
> H - short exchange with the section team mate

We have already looked at the principle movements in preceding sections. At this point, I wish only to stress the importance of the change of play, describing two examples - and I would also like to suggest two further options.

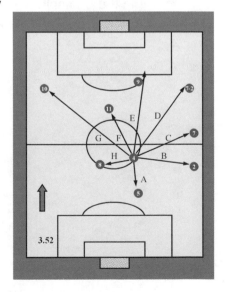

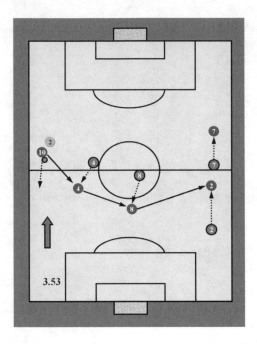

3.53

CHANGE OF PLAY: in fig. 3.53 we can see a well-thought out change of play. The left side mid fielder, 10, is being pressed and he sends the ball diagonally to 4, who gives it on to 8, who has in the meantime carried out a diagonal backward movement. After having passed the ball, 10 returns towards his mid field, and the side mid fielder on the opposite flank, 7, creates depth, allowing 2 to move up. In the example, 8 carries out a pass to the side defender as he is moving forward.

In Fig. 3.54, after having tried in vain to break through on the right with a combination between 8, 9 and 7, the team decides to move back and regroup: 8 offers himself for a pass, receives it and sends it straight to the other flank towards 10, the far side mid fielder.

When we have put a lot of effort into play on one side of the field, it is a good idea to change play as quickly as possible, so that the opposing defenders do not have the time for their horizontal shifts.

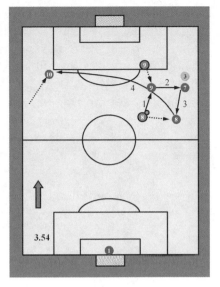

SIDE OVERLAPPING: an example is given in the maneuver shown in Fig. 3.55. Play begins from the defense; 6 passes to 2, who widens out to 7. 7 decides to move towards the center with the ball, giving the center mid fielder, 8, the opportunity to carry out an external overlap by passing behind him. 7 gives the ball to 11, who widens out to the sides as 8 runs up. 8 crosses so that 9 can shoot. When 8 begins his overlapping move, his section team mate 4 and the left side mid fielder 10 tighten in towards the right to give coverage.

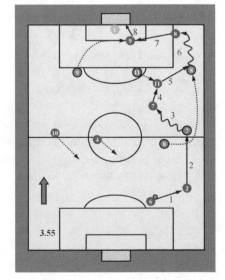

BREAKING INTO THE CENTER: this is an effective movement, frequently used by teams who do not have offensive side players. As shown in Fig. 3.56, the moment that 4 passes to 9, who is moving to meet him, mid fielder 8 sprints into depth receiving 9's rebound pass. At this point he can have a shot at goal or pass the ball into depth to striker 11.

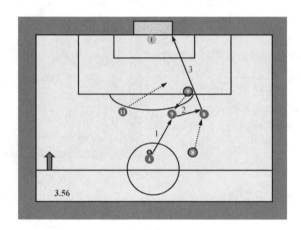

3.56

MOVEMENTS OF THE DEFENSE

More and more frequently in modern soccer, the defense is expected to take an active part in the team's attacking phase. Having less and less time to carry out our plays, it becomes indispensable to find free space. It can, therefore, be decisive both on a technical and a psychological level for a mid fielder to have the option of making a backward pass towards a team mate who is in a position to start the build up facing the opponent's goal.

You have to use whatever free spaces there may be, and it is of the utmost importance in this light to exploit the whole width of the field, trying, therefore, to create situations of numerical superiority on the sidelines. That is why, particularly with regard to the 4-4-2 system, the side defenders must move up and cooperate continually with the mid fielders.

Center defenders

Because of the position in which they are placed, these are the players that have the most complete vision of what is taking place on the field. They are also normally allowed a certain liberty of movement. In fact, the opposing team will very probably not be able to sustain ultra-offensive pressing for the whole period of the match.
It goes without saying that having at least one center defender in the team who is capable of setting up play will give fluidity to the attacking maneuvers.
The determining factor is the support that they give to the mid fielders: a mid fielder in difficulty must know that he can count on support from the defenders behind him, and that he can be fully confident of how they will manage the ball the moment he makes the back pass.

One of the fundamental resources of at least one of the two central defenders is his ability in the air, and this is decisive following on offensive development from set plays, these being occasions which more and more often influence the results of a match.
In Fig. 3.57 we have shown the main passing lines stemming from a center defender in possession: he can send the ball to a section team mate or to a mid fielder who is suitably free of marking. If he is being pressed, he can make a back pass towards his goalkeeper - in that case, however, it is better if the pass is directed away from the goal mouth.

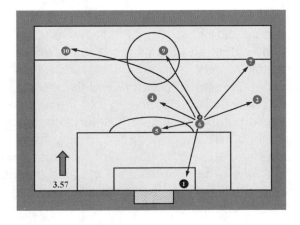

3.57

Another important quality is precision in the long pass, with which the player can send the ball directly to the striker over the heads of the mid field. This solution can be productive where there is a first striker on the field who is able to control such passes and then choose whether to dump the ball quickly on the second striker or to protect it, allowing the team to move up and re compact.

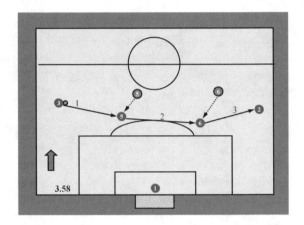

Fig. 3.58 illustrates a situation of play that very often comes about during a match, i.e., the passage of the ball from one side of the field to the other in the defense area. It is vital to coach all the members of the defense section so that they can carry out such operations quickly and precisely.

In cases like this, any interception of the ball would be disastrous, and so once again it is a good idea not to pass horizontally, though of course this will also depend on the distances at which the opposing strikers are placed.

In the 4-4-2, it is the side defenders' job to move up and collaborate with the mid fielders and teams more rarely expect central defenders to break into space in front. Personally, however, I feel that this second option should be more widely used to vary play and give it less predictability. By moving into the mid field, a central defender could put the opposition's defense organization in serious difficulty in a very important zone of play, forcing them into a situation of numerical inferiority. Our own team would not be put out of balance either, especially if the side defenders know that in circumstances like these they must remain in coverage and tighten in alongside the other center defender, practically creating a three-man defense. The defender can break into space with or without the ball. You can see two examples in Fig. 3.59 and 3.60.

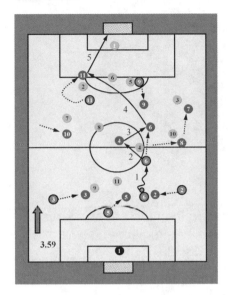
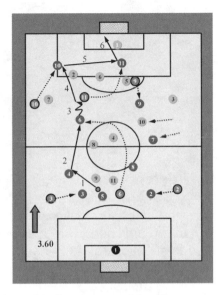

In the first, 6 is in possession, and, not being pressed by the opposing strikers, he decides to advance with the ball. 3 and 2 immediately tighten in towards the center to 5's side, and they move up together - a couple of yards towards the mid field line. The side mid fielder, 7, creates depth and 8 moves wide to take up the space that has been vacated, so allowing 6 to break in. 10 tightens in to cover. When he gets to the mid field line, 6 goes for a one, two exchange with 4, and then passes to 11, who has just completed an L-shaped movement in the area. 7's movement is important as well because he forces the opposition's defense to stay wide.

Fig. 3.60 shows a movement without the ball. 4 comes down diagonally towards the left to receive the ball from 5. 6 decides to move into depth and 2, 3 and 5 form a compact three- man line. When he gets past the opposing center mid fielder (four), 6 suddenly changes direction towards the left, cutting in behind him and receives the vertical pass from his team mate. Seeing that 6 is coming towards him, 10 gives him space moving up along the sidelines, while the other side mid fielder, 7, tightens in to cover. 6 advances with the ball for a yard or two forcing the defenders to come out, and then passes to 10, who has got round the defense. He shoots or passes to a striker in the center.

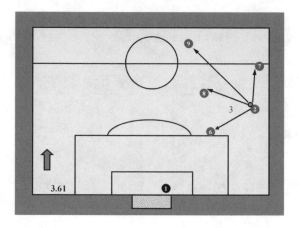

Side defenders

The side defenders have an important role in the attacking system of a team lined up with the 4-4-2. Their movements will often lead to situations of numerical superiority along the sidelines. Along with their ability in defense, they will also need good stamina and technical aptitude. The side defenders must be able to develop their skill at crossing while in movement, and these crosses need to be both tense and precise.
In Fig. 3.61 we have set out the most important passing lines that can be made by a side defender when he is in possession: his options are a diagonal backward pass towards the center defender, a pass to the center mid fielder, widening out along the sidelines to the side mid fielder and, lastly, a direct pass to a striker. This last alternative is widely used when the opponents are pressing the mid fielders, and it allows the striker who has come to meet it to rebound on a center mid fielder or to widen out to the flank for a side player. We can now have a look at the main developments connected with the participation of the side defenders.

ONE - TWO: a very simple play, as shown in Fig. 3.62. 7 lengthens the team along the sidelines, allowing 2 to move up with the ball at his feet. Near the opponent, 2 makes a triangular play with the nearest center mid fielder. This is an easy play, but it is also delicate because it is absolutely vital that opponent n° ten does not intercept the pass towards 8. In any case the team must be ready to intervene if the interception should take place, and so 6, 5 and 3 will shift towards the right and 10 will tighten in to cover. When he has received the return pass, 2 will have a number of possibilities open to him, including the one shown in the example: a sudden inside cut followed by a vertical pass on 11's movement. 11 then shoots at goal.

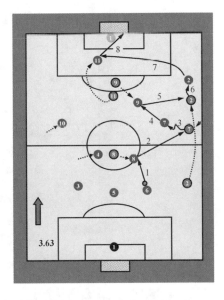

OVERLAPPING ON THE SIDELINES: this is a classic offensive play, built up by the players in the side chain. In Fig. 3.63, 8 receives from 6 and widens out onto the flank to 7, who runs in with the ball inviting 2 to overlap on the sidelines. 9 makes a move in support of 7, receives the pass and rebounds to the side to meet 2 running up. 2 crosses and 11 should be on the near post after having made an L-shaped movement. After passing to the sidelines, 9 should go towards the far post.

INTERNAL OVERLAPPING: this is shown in Fig. 3.64. As you can see, 3 carries out a movement without the ball, leaving the left side mid fielder between him and the sideline. 3 begins this movement when he notices that 10 is on the sideline and 4 is about to pass him the ball. As a consequence, 5, 6 and 2 shift towards the left to cover.

Having used this play to escape the opposing mid fielder's (seven) contrast, 3 now receives the ball from 10 and can continue the action.

In the figure, we show an internal triangular exchange with 11, which will bring 3 to the shot from the edge of the penalty area.

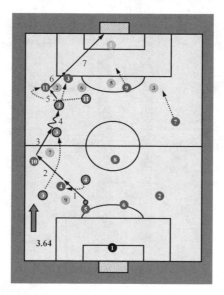

3.64

THE GOALKEEPER

I will now conclude these considerations concerning the players' movements in applying the 4-4-2 system with a brief note about the goalkeeper.

In the recent past, following the introduction of the rule that does not allow the goalkeeper to block the ball with his hands after a voluntary back pass from a team mate, the preparation of the n° one has necessarily undergone various modifications. It now happens quite frequently that the goalkeeper has to use his feet to kick the ball away, and we must not underrate the technical difficulty of such a play. The results are already clear to see: and contrary to what used to happen some time ago, it is now quite rare to see a goalkeeper bungle a kick.

This is a useful thing, naturally, so much so that in recent times we often see the goalkeeper controlling the ball and turning play towards the center or side defender.

This change has important consequences for teams that use zonal play and techniques like pressing and offside, because the goalkeeper will now be expected to take part in the play with his feet as well.

As we can see in Fig. 3.65, when the defense line moves up in a block to shorten up towards the mid fielders and keep the team short, the goalkeeper must come out and place himself at the edge of the penalty area, ready to intervene in the case of any long passes from the opposing team. He must be prepared, technically and psychologically, to act as the last man and to anticipate the opponent's strikers when and if they take the defense by surprise. He must of course be in possession of the basics of playing on the ground.

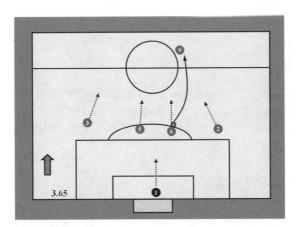

ATTACKING SOLUTIONS

The many examples that we have described and set out in their relative illustrations should give a complete outline of the numerous attacking developments guaranteed by the 4-4-2. There are, naturally, many variations on the plays we have been presenting, but these are the general principles that regulate the organized movements to be carried out by the team.

Time after time the coach will have to choose which are the best for his team, basing himself on the strengths of his own players and taking into account the peculiarities of the side he is about to face.

At a professional level, this sport has reached a very high degree of preparation from a technical, tactical and physical point of view. Coaches can find a quantity of detailed information about adversaries and they can set up effective countermeasures to limit the dangers these represent in attack.

I am convinced that the best way to put any defense system into difficulty - always with consideration to the quality of the players on our side - is to give great variation to our attacking solutions. This attitude forces the defense to face many different situations of play, and it will give a clear vision of any of their possible shortcomings.

In addition, it also increases the unpredictability of the maneuvers. It goes without saying that it is very useful to have one or two players on the team who are gifted with great technical abilities and imagination.

BUILDING UP PLAY

This is the definition we give to the attacking phase when we are trying to get near our opponents' goal.

There are two main categories: reasoned build up and rapid build up.

The first is based on elaborate movements, a number of short passes that allow the members of the team to move up with the ball. Here, we need above average technical skills combined with a good level of collective organization.

Rapid build up on the other hand foresees the systematic use of long passes towards the strikers or an in-depth side player with offensive skills. We can use this method only if we have players on the field who are able to make precise long passes, and, above all, attacking players able to control passes coming directly from behind and then to bring the team up and finalize the play in collaboration with the section team mate.

You can also used mixed build up, i.e., avoid in depth pressing with a long pass and start elaborate play from the mid field line or from the opponent's three quarters. In this case, defenders and mid fielders must move quickly into depth following the long pass in order to receive their attacking players' dumps or to intervene when the opponents gain possession or clear.

Reasoned build up

We must develop skill in ball possession, and it will be necessary to do technical exercises to perfect our speed and precision in ball control and short passing.

Another important skill that the players must possess is positioning themselves on the field in order to facilitate a pass from the player in possession. The principles to be coached are the ability to create and attack space, not to mention the habit of using the whole width of the field.

You can develop the players' ability to place themselves in a rational way on the field from a point of view that is slightly different from the one that we have just set out. This consists in giving the team the ability to outline geometric figures like the triangle or a rhombus on the ground as a result of the players' own dynamism. During the development of the action, the players should create the points of geometrical triangular shapes (and consequently of a quadrilateral form, if you are talking about two triangles that have a side in common as shown in Fig. 3.66). This type of set up is very effective, because it assures the player in possession of a number of easy solutions. In Fig. 3.66, we show a good movement carried out by a center mid fielder in order, as we have already said, to free himself of marking by making a backward diagonal cut before receiving the ball from the defenders. It will be clear how this effectively forms triangles in that part of the field (and quadrilateral shapes as in the one whose angles are represented by 3, 4, 8 and 5).

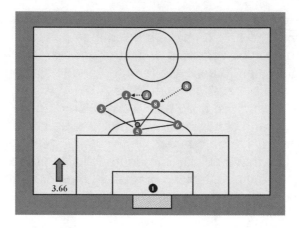

3.66

Generally speaking, two lines that are close together, like, for example, the defense and the mid field, should never be straight, i.e., the players should not be aligned vertically, but should create a number of triangles on the ground. To tell the truth, this is not always possible to carry out and can sometimes appear strained. It is more natural to move in by following the guidelines of how to create and occupy space, which in themselves will very often guarantee the triangular set up (cf. the example in Fig. 3.66, where 8 begins to free himself of marking and 4 opens up the space by making a diagonal movement to the right). Fig. 3.67 shows one of the many exercises used for getting players into the habit of drawing up triangles on the field. 4, 7 and 8 are placed as a triangle; 4 at the apex furthest back is in possession. He passes to a team mate, 7 in the example, and then chooses how and when to move. As a consequence, 8, who has not received the ball, will have to move as well in order to form a new triangle.

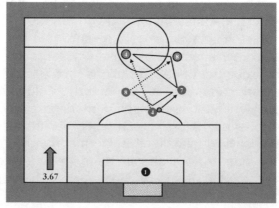

3.67

You can do a whole lot of exercises, but they all have two fundamental principles: a player who does not receive the ball must
move in relation to the player who carried out the pass (for example, if 4 did not move, 8 would have to make a short diagonal forward movement in order to receive the ball; if 7 then passed it to
him, 4 would then move forward leaving 7 as the bottom apex);
also, you must always have one player behind covering the others.

As we have already mentioned above, in addition to technical
and group exercises like those we have just described, we must
coach the possession phase by playing matches between two
teams whose only aim is ball possession. The area of the field
will depend on the number of players on each side and the skills
you want them to develop. If, for example you want the team to
acquire the habit of keeping calm when the opponents are pressing, you will need a crowded field. Lastly, it is useful to get the
team to play in numerical disparity.

At this point, I would like to make a consideration: teams wishing
to impose their play will have to use effective offensive pressing
in order to keep the ball in their opponent's half. Having regained
possession, the most widely used weapon will be the rapid counterattack, i.e., short attacking plays that often involve a number of
players, and which set off from an advanced part of the field.
This is undeniably very tiring from a physical point of view, and
teams will probably not be able to keep it up for the whole match.
It is necessary, therefore, to slow down every so often, keeping
possession as long as we are able, and alternating elaborate
passing movements with sudden vertical passes. In Fig. 3.68
there is an exercise you can use to coach an attitude like this. It
is a match, 7 against 7 with only one goal. The playing field is the
area between the two areas delimited lengthwise by prolonging
the short side of the area (cf. figure). The field is divided into
three zones and the two teams face each other in zone B. They
must carry out a series of six consecutive passes, and from that
moment on they can pass no more than three more times (you
can also set a time limit) in order to free a man of marking in
zone C and set him up for a shot. When the sixth pass has been
carried out, a player from each team can enter zone A. The

member of the team in possession has to get himself free of
marking in order to receive the
ball in zone C, while the other
has to remain in zone A and
must try to intercept the vertical
pass without moving into zone C.

Vary play even during the same
match: ball possession and vertical passes, side attacks and central assault, change of play - this
is the recipe for creating problems even for a very well-prepared defense.
I will now give you a detailed
illustration of a number of plays which, setting off from the
defense, evolve through a series of short passes exploiting the
collaboration among different chains of players.

SIDE CHAIN: Fig. 3.69 is an
illustration of a double external
overlap involving two side players, a mid fielder and a striker.
The center defender, 5, passes
to 4, who, not being pressed,
moves up towards the mid field,
seeks a one-two exchange with
his section team mate, 8, and
then passes to 9. He rebounds
onto the other striker who has
just completed a cut. 11 receives
the ball in the area and shoots at
goal.

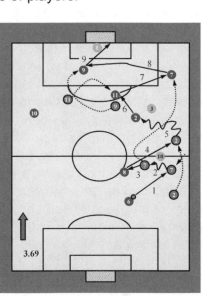

CENTRAL CHAIN: Fig. 3.70 shows a play that starts and ends in the center, and which requires the cooperation of the two center mid fielders and the two strikers. The center back 5 passes to 4, who, as he is not being pressed, moves up with the ball towards the mid field, goes for a one two with his section team mate 8, and then passes to 9. 9 rebounds immediately onto the other striker who has made a cut; 11 receives the ball in the area and takes a shot.

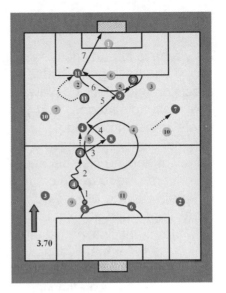

3.70

CHANGE OF FLANK: as in Fig. 3.71. The defense is passing the ball around until the right side mid fielder, 10, gets posses-

sion. He is closely pressed and decides to place the ball with a backward diagonal pass towards 4. A rapid combination 4-9-8-7 frees the last man in this series. 7 crosses to the center and a striker shoots.

Note the placement of the players creating the many triangles on the field (the various apexes are the players themselves), which is a confirmation of how well space is being covered.

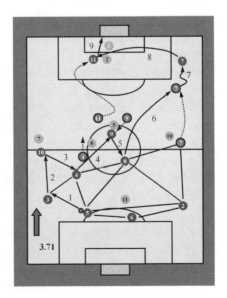

3.71

Rapid build up

As we have already pointed out this is a useful attacking solution only if you have players able to make 40-50 yard passes with precision and attacking players capable of receiving them.
The main advantage is that you will be able to elude the opponents' in-depth pressing.
It is indispensable to have a tower who is particularly strong in the air, if nothing else because long passes give opposing defenders time to get into suitable positions and to anticipate. An alternative to the tower would be the presence of strikers who are particularly good at gaining space and who can prevent the opposition from anticipating. Another important thing is the speed with which the team mates supply support.
Having controlled the ball in the opponent's half, by no means an easy operation, the attacking front can play for time, protecting the ball and allowing the defenders and mid fielders to come up behind, after which the finalizing maneuvers will begin. In this case, if it is a fairly elaborate action which brings the team into position for the shot on goal, then we are talking of mixed build up, because, in one single phase of possession it involves a long pass over the heads of the mid field followed by a series of short passes.
Sometimes immediate build up can lead to an equally rapid shot on goal. This happens when the strikers receive the pass from behind and, without waiting for their team mates' support, set up a quick action finishing up with a shot on goal. Teams that are relying heavily on this type of solution should make sure that the side mid fielders take turns positioning themselves in depth so that the final plays will be able to count on the participation of three players.

There is an example in 3.72. The center defender, 6, passes into depth looking for 9. Just before the striker touches the ball, 10 makes a cut below him in order to receive the rebound; he passes to the other striker, 11, beyond the defense line.

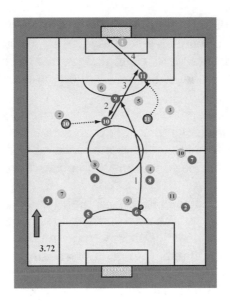

3.72

FINALIZING PLAY

We have set out the movements of the attack in detail above. Here, I would like to consider for a moment how important it is when coaching a team to prepare the players to affront the greatest possible number of situations that they will be meeting in the match. During a match, other factors like tension and physical exhaustion can have a negative effect on the team's reactions, and so it is useful, when the players a good technical level, to carry out exercises that reproduce as faithfully as possible the kind of thing they will be facing during a competition.
It is important to look after questions like how to make use of set plays: free kicks, corners, the throw in from the sides and penalties. You shouldn't neglect the position to take up to recover clearing passes from the opposing defense or from the goalkeeper.
During a match the team should be able to detect the weaknesses of the opposing team and then use them to its own advantage.
You must be able to attack beginning from any sector of the field. A useful exercise is to place a team on the field, without opponents to start with, and have the attack begin from the defense, then from the flank, from the opponent's three quarters, from

when the ball is put in from the sides, etc. The next step is to try out different types of offensive solutions, breaking in to the center, getting around defenders, changing play, rapid build up ... At this point we put opponents on the field, first in numerical inferiority, then in equality.

Teams that wish to carry out offensive pressing must pay special attention to counterattacking, bringing up situations in which they have to regain possession in the opponent's half and making sure the players are able to interpret the positive transition phase.

You must connect exercises in pressing and counterattacking: two teams, 9 against 11 face each other on the whole field. You ask the team in numerical superiority to go into offensive pressing (paying particular attention to invited pressing), which will call for transition and rapid counterattacking.

You must also do exercises in attacking with numerical superiority, so that you can make the best use of such advantageous situations.

In Fig. 3.73 and 3.74 we can see two different solutions for a 3 against 2 attack. In Fig. 3.73, the center player is in possession; the two defenders must play for time and be ready to go into depth to leave a striker offside should he go over the line of the ball. The attacking players' aim is to go from a 3 against 2 situation to a 2 against 1.

Player 9 moves up, ball at his feet, until a defender is forced to come out to meet him. At that moment, to avoid offside, 9 passes to 10, who has moved into the space left free by the defender. The player in possession can also try to create a 2 against 1 by going for an opponent and setting up a one-two exchange with the nearest team mate.

In Fig. 3.74, a side player advances with the ball. Defender n° six will move towards him and 9 cuts in behind. If defender five follows him as in the diagram, 10 then passes to 7, who shoots. On the contrary, if five plays for time, 10 must make a good vertical pass to 9 before he finishes up beyond the two defenders.

It often happens that a match is resolved by the skills of a single player. The coach must keep this in mind and organize teams that will put such qualities into light. For example, if there is a player on the team who is particularly good at dribbling, it is important to create one against one situations, in which he can

4-4-2

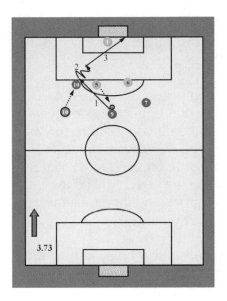

3.73

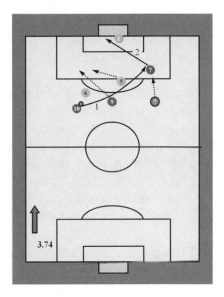

3.74

show his ability.

In Fig. 3.75 we show a play that can create a 1 against 1 situation along the left flank. The ball goes from the left side of the defense towards the right part of the mid field. The opponent's defense will start to shift in that direction and this attitude will be further accentuated if the two strikers and the right side mid fielder carry out movements to widen out play on the strong side. In the example, 11 cuts towards the right, 9 goes in support of 8 who is in possession and 7 places himself on his own sideline. The opposing defenders three, five and six will invariably be attracted towards the strong side. The strikers' and 7's movements are made in order to free space on the left flank, where 10 must be fast enough to present himself for 8's change of play. Only defender two is likely to be able to get back into position, while his team mates will not be capable of assuring him cover. So we now have a one against one situation between the left

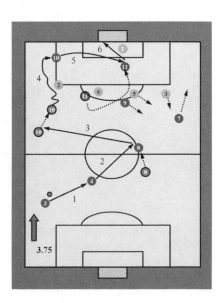

3.75

side mid fielder, 10, and the defender, two. Depending on the type of dribbling he carries out (along the sidelines or towards the center), 10 will cross or shoot directly at goal.

I conclude this analysis of the attacking phase using the 4-4-2 system by underlining the importance of preparing the team so as to get the active participation of all the players. The coach will have to move ahead step by step, giving the players exercises that get steadily more difficult. At the same time, he must stimulate their critical spirit - at the beginning the coach will be the one to speak, later he will limit himself to presenting the problems, which the players themselves will have to resolve.

The team must assimilate the basic principles of play and make them their own so that they can react collectively and in an organized way to every obstacle or predicament.
When you have reached this level of play, it becomes important to stimulate individual initiatives - above all in the most imaginative players and those most gifted from a technical point of view - so that the team is able to respond in a unified way to personal plays that have not been planned, but which have the important advantage of greatly increasing the unpredictability of our maneuvers.

CHAPTER 4

THE 4-4-2 AGAINST OTHER PLAYING SYSTEMS

Luca Prestigiacomo

CONTRASTING YOUR OPPONENT'S SYSTEM

When our team lined up with the 4-4-2 has to face opponents organized in other systems or even with the same system that we are using, it is a good idea to adopt tactical adjustments that will enable us to contrast them.
Setting up against an opponent's system involves invalidating their points of force and exploiting their weaknesses. In order to do this, the counter moves that we make must cancel out the positive aspects of the playing system we are facing especially in the offensive phase, and underline its defects, in particular in the defense phase.

In the defense phase we must try to force our opponents to play where they find it most difficult, trying to shift in such a way as to best oppose their typical set up. In relation to the natural place-ment of the players on the field, we will have to decide where and with which players to carry out good doubling up of marking with the greatest continuity.
We will also have to imagine what offensive plays will be most frequently used by the team we are facing depending on its play-ing system, so that we can adopt the necessary countermea-sures to inhibit their normal movements.

As far as the offensive phase is concerned, we have to establish first of all whether it is better to hit them by using depth for the most part, or the width of the playing field. As a consequence, we will then decide what finishing touch techniques to put into effect in order to get into a position to shoot at goal. For example, against an opponent that is having problems along the sidelines, we will attempt to get into position for a shot by using crosses or overlapping on the flanks; while if our adversaries have more dif-ficulty in the center, the best finishing touches to use will be cuts or dump and rebound passes.
In the phase of possession we will also use plays that permit us to exploit the situations of numerical superiority that come out as a result of the placement of the team on the field. In addition, we will have to try to create numerical superiority in parts of the field where we are in numerical equality.
By creating and employing these situations of numerical

supremacy we will be able to gain space in front because we will be making constant use of uncontrolled players to receive passes and open spaces to attack. This means that the opponents will be forced to shift when the ball is not in movement so as to rule out these situations of numerical inferiority; thus, it will be easier for us to develop maneuvers in the direction of the opposition's goal or even pass to a team mate in the area who is free of marking.

As far as developing the maneuvers is concerned, we must always try to bring the whole team up with the ball without ever using the long pass against any adversary. Reasoned build up is much more effective, as well as being more spectacular, because the team remains short and compact. On the contrary, when using the long pass, the team loosens up and there is every like-lihood that the ball will end up in the defenders' possession, for they are without any doubt at an advantage in this sort of long range play. You should use the long pass only in an emergency situation, i.e., when a defender is in difficulty because he is being pressed and has no other solution than to carry out a forward pass to alleviate the danger.

We can also use the long pass in cases where the opposing defense is badly placed, and, having one or two attacking players free, it seems a good idea for us to get the ball to them at once. It is also important to remember that it is the players themselves who must decide, on the basis of the tactical situation and the part of the field in which we have regained possession, whether it is better to go for an immediate counterattack (with the ball on the ground) or whether it might be a good idea to set up a more elaborate maneuver.

In order to decide which tactical ploys to use against the oppo-nents in a particular match, we must first of all evaluate the 'numerical situations' that will crop up in the various parts of the field. This means that we must not look at the numerical situation only from the point of view of the single sections, but, above all, in relation to the flanks and the central zones of the field (center of the defense, center of the mid field, center of the attack).

On this basis, we will decide how to act in the offense phase, and how to shift in the phase of non-possession, what finishing touch techniques to use most frequently and in which zones to put doubling up of marking into effect with the greatest continuity.

It is also important to note whether our opponents use zonal play or man marking so as to decide what movements the strikers should carry out most often. If the opponent is using the zone, the strikers will make greater use of cuts, combinations and movements of the type 'two go, one comes'. If the opponents are man marking, the strikers will mainly be carrying out crossovers and deviations.

It is clear that we will not be able to give full treatment to the subject without knowing all we can about the characteristics of the players on the opposing team. It is important to know which opposing players are more skilled in dribbling, who is the director of the team, which players are the points of reference for their team mates and who will find himself in greatest difficulty when being pressed - all this will help us prepare our tactical countermoves for the match. As a consequence, we will devise the systematic doubling up of marking on players capable of creating numerical superiority by dribbling, we will attempt to put their playing front under constant pressure and we will set up situations of invited pressing so as to force the rival player in possession to pass the ball to his less technically gifted team mates or to those who have particular problems when they are being pressed.

The coach's aim should be to create tactical organization that can be considered universal. This means that the team must be capable of resolving any situation that may come up on the field, moving with precision in reaction to whatever plays the opponents happen to be making. Players must be 'situationally' educated. They must have grasped their tactics and the various plays in such a way that they can put them into practice in concrete situations. This will also make the coach's job much easier: he will not need to dedicate much time to preparing each match, explaining time after time how to deal with a three-man defense, how to deal with cuts, with overlapping, etc. The coach must avoid becoming too tactically obsessive, trying to turn soccer matches into games of chess. What he must do is give simple suggestions to the players on how to behave against a particular side, dedicating the rest of the time to perfecting the universal tactical organization that will give him a team that is both instinctive and aware.

The mentality of the team must always be the same, just as the system and the playing style must always be put into effect with rhythm and decision against whatever opponent. A single match will bring variations to some of the movements in both phases of play, but these must not alter the way the team faces the situation. The team must always be fast, dynamic, aggressive, offensive and, of course, spectacular.

THE 4-4-2 AGAINST THE 4-4-2

When playing against the 4-4-2, it goes without saying that the two teams reflect each other. In the mid field we are 4 against 4, in defense 4 against 2 and in attack 2 against 4. We are in numerical equality (2 against 2) on both flanks, and the situation is the same everywhere in the center (2 against 2 in the center of the defense, 2 against 2 in the mid field, 2 against 2 at the center of the attack). This is clearly laid out in figure 4.1. It is easy to think that this match will be full of 'duels' between pairs of players: our two center defenders against the two strikers, our two right side players against their left side players, our two left side players against their right side players, our two center mid fielders against theirs and our two strikers against their two center defenders.

In some cases these situations of numerical equality are to our disadvantage, some are favorable and others are indifferent to us. In fact, the 2 against 2 of our center defenders against their two strikers represents a danger, while our strikers' 2 against 2 with their central defenders is to our advantage and the numerical equality in the center of the mid field and along the sidelines is to nobody's true benefit. Generally speaking, our task is to make the most of the favorable 2 against 2 situation in attack, to avoid the 2 against 2 in the center of our defense and to turn the other situations of numerical equality to our advantage.

As well as that, we should make sure the team is moving around in a compact way, creating numerical superiority everywhere on the field.

As the two systems are identical we must concentrate on our psychological approach in order to get the better of our opponents - on our tactical organization and our athletic preparation. Clearly, also individual tactical skills must also be counted as an

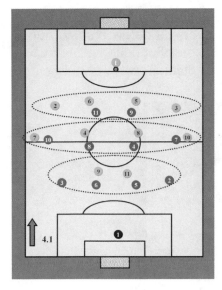

4.1

important element which can topple the balance created, on paper at least, by two teams using the same system. We will now have a look at both the defense and the offense phase to point out moves that will allow us to exploit our opponent's weaknesses on the one hand and the difficulties that our system will be facing on the other.

The attacking phase

In the attacking phase we will have to exploit the natural 2 against 2 set up as our strikers go in against their center defenders. The important thing is to stop their side backs from becoming useful in the center; keeping them occupied on the flanks with our two side mid fielders, who will have to play in depth. In this way, we will create a global 4 against 4 situation in attack, which will mean that their defense is stretched out and under pressure on the sidelines. They will then be playing in what is called 'system purity', i.e., in numerical equality man against man. At this point, we must play

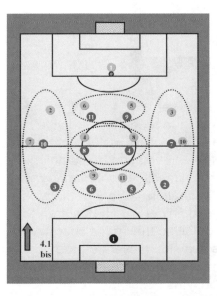

4.1
bis

the ball on one of our two strikers, who will look at once for his section team mate to shoot, exploiting combinations as the finishing touch technique.

With these triangular plays between the two strikers there is every chance that we will be able to free one from the control of the center defender, which means that he will then be isolated. To better exploit this situation in attack, it is important to try to change the 2 against 2 into a 3 against 2 in our favor. Trying to get numerical superiority against their center defenders is of fundamental importance in getting the better of opponents lined up with the 4-4-2. There are a number of different ways of going

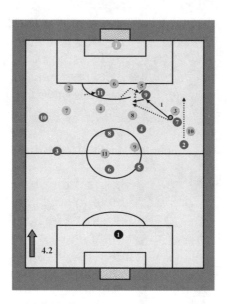

Give and follow, side mid fielder - striker (Fig. 4.2). When he has passed to the striker who has come to meet him, the side mid fielder cuts internally downfield of the striker instead of sprinting into depth. The striker finishes the combination by dumping on the side mid fielder, who now finds himself free of marking. Here we have created a 3 against 2 situation. Note that the side defender on the same flank as the mid fielder who has set up the play has also sprinted into depth, exploiting the space liberated by his team mate's cut in. Also, the two side players on the opposite flank have also moved up to make sure that their defender on the weak side is being kept as busy as possible.

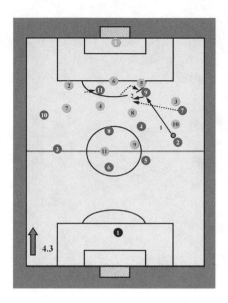

The side mid fielder cuts in 'under' the strikers, with the side defender in possession. Our side defender has the ball and the side mid fielder on the same flank makes an internal cut under the strikers. The nearest striker comes to meet the side defender for the rebound onto the side mid fielder, who receives the ball creating a 3 against 2 situation at the center of the attacking front (Fig. 4.3).

A center mid fielder advances. This can take place in two ways. In the first case, the side mid fielder is in possession and the center mid fielder nearest to him comes up and then moves back a yard or two to give support; the other center mid fielder then advances to act as a sort of attacking mid fielder. Our side player in possession can now pass into depth on the center mid fielder, and we can exploit a 3 to 2 situation against their center defenders.

Secondly, we can play the ball onto one of the two strikers who has come to meet the player in possession; he will then dump towards the corresponding center mid fielder who has come up in time to act as support. The center mid fielder now in possession has created a 3 to 2 situation against the two center defenders. The inside mid fielder could even carry out a central overlapping move without limiting himself as a mere support. In this way you put the opposing center defender in a 1 against 2 situation.

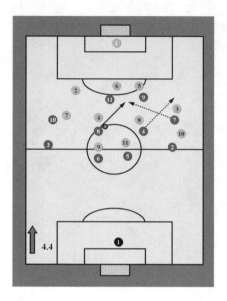

4.4

***Interchange of position in the mid field between a side and
center player.*** A center mid fielder is in possession, and there is
a crossover between the other internal mid fielder and the side
player nearest to him. The former center mid fielder is now positioned on the flank, while the one time side player is placed centrally on the three quarters. If he receives the ball straight away, it
will create a situation of numerical superiority (Fig. 4.4).

All these favorable 3 to 2 situations against the opposition's central defenders must be exploited in the best way possible. A player finding himself in possession in front of the two rival center
backs must move ahead, exploiting the space that has been created for him. If one of the two center defenders comes out to
close him off, one of our attacking players must be free to receive
the ball in the penalty area. If neither of the opposing defenders
comes out, our player in possession will move on, until, finding
himself in the penalty area, he will be able to take advantage of
the situation personally by shooting at goal.
The strikers' 'one comes, one goes' movements are very important. They open gaps in the heart of the opponent's defense,
which can then be attacked by a third player.
Playing against a 4-4-2 we will also need to dominate on the
flanks in order to finish off the play by making a cross from the
bottom line. The two pairs of side players will have to work tire-

lessly, carrying out continuous overlapping movements to get past the opposition presented by the corresponding defenders. In order to make life seriously difficult for our opponents on the flanks we will have to create situations of numerical superiority here also. That must come about by having a third player participate in plays along the flanks.

This third player could be a striker moving wide or a center mid fielder breaking in.

We will now have a look at some alternatives for creating numerical superiority along the sidelines.

A center mid fielder breaks into play along the sidelines.

With a side defender in possession, the side mid fielder goes to meet him, so attracting the rival side defender. At once the center mid fielder takes up the space left free, and, having cleared himself of marking, receives the ball. A center defender will have to move in on him, forcing the whole section to shift towards the flank. This will probably leave one of the strikers free to receive the ball, or, in any case, we could now have empty spaces in the center to be attacked from behind. In Fig 4.5 we can also see the shifting move of the other center mid fielder to take the place of his section team mate breaking into the side. Even the side mid fielder on the opposite flank has tightened his position.

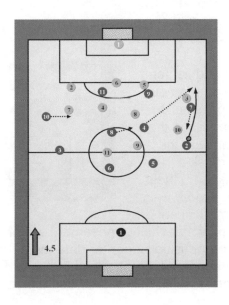

A center mid fielder breaks into play along the sidelines.
With a side defender in possession, the side mid fielder widens out, turning his back to the sideline. While the ball is moving from the side defender to the side mid fielder, the nearest center defender breaks into the flank, positioning himself as a wing. The side mid fielder passes on to him as soon as he has received the ball, sprinting immediately into depth in order to carry out an instant overlapping move. This play will probably create problems for the opponent's defense, who will have to carry out complicated shifting moves, which will allow us to put a player in position to shoot at goal.

Interchange of position between a side and a center mid fielder (Fig. 4.6). With a side defender in possession, the side mid fielder cuts in towards the center, freeing space to be attacked by the insertion of a center mid fielder. The side back passes to him at once as he breaks in. This play is an excellent example of collective movements to create and attack space.

Deviation of a striker. A side mid fielder is in possession, pressed by an opposing side back. The striker widens out towards the sidelines (flag post movement). At the same time, our side defender needs to overlap to put their side defender in a 1 to 3 situation. If their side mid fielder was about to double up on our side mid fielder in possession, he will now have to exchange the marking on our man with the ball. Our overlapping side defender will be taken by their side defender. And so, we will in any case be in numerical superi-

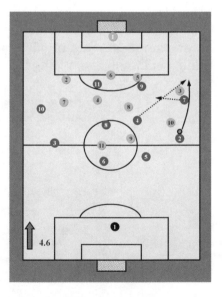

ority 3 to 2. The striker's deviating movement will probably have attracted one of the opposition's center defenders, creating space in the middle. This space will be attacked by the other striker with a cut to break in, or by a mid fielder inserting himself a moment later or even by the side mid fielder in possession, who will attack the space in the center carrying out a give and follow with the striker.

When facing a 4-4-2, you must remember that one of the characteristics of this system is to carry out pressing with continuity, and consequently doubling up on marking and using offside tactics. Our team must be ready to affront our opponent's probable in-depth pressing. In order to do this the mid fielders and the strikers need to move around without the ball all the time so as to help our defenders when they are in trouble. The mobility of all the team members is vital to get over the problem of pressing - as are changes of play towards parts of the field where there are fewer opponents. Note also that the center defenders must continuously open play towards the side defenders who will probably have more space and give a sure outlet for our maneuvers. Concerning double teaming, the 4-4-2 calls for persistent collaboration between pairs of players on the vertical plane, i.e., each defender should be able to count on help from a mid fielder. In this sense, each side defender is assisted by his corresponding side mid fielder and each center defender is sustained by the corresponding center mid fielder.

As a consequence, when they receive the ball, our strikers will be closed off by a center defender and an internal mid fielder will be doubling up. To avoid this, our center mid fielders must be ready to move up in support of the strikers, who will be able to dump on them immediately so that the ball is still ahead of the position from which it was kicked.

On the flanks, their side mid fielder will be doubling up on ours in collaboration with their side defender; it is enough that our side defender overlaps with the mid fielder and they will not be able to carry out the double team.

If our opponents are using offside tactics, we must insert players from the back ready to receive balls undisturbed when their defense is not quick enough to move back and carry out the correct shift. The strikers will move back so as not to finish up in an offside position, but, as soon as they can, they must be ready to make divergent cuts with crescent movements.

To sum up, when you are attacking the 4-4-2 you must alternate side and central attacks, attempting time and again to create numerical superiority against their center and side defenders. As a result, the finishing up techniques put into use will have to be crosses from the base line, combinations and dump and rebound passes.

The defense phase

We must expect our opponents to use the same offensive moves as us during our phase of non-possession. We must expect them to:

- Try to exploit the 2 against 2 with our two central defenders.
- Make an attempt to create a 3 to 2 against our center defenders.
- Try to create a situation of numerical superiority along the sidelines.

In order to avoid numerical equality in the center of the defense, it is a good idea for the four defenders to keep tight so that the two side defenders offer some help in the center.
Keep in mind that the opponent's side players will be playing in depth so as to set up a 4 to 4 against our defense, putting our side players under pressure. In any case, our side defenders should keep tight, ready to close off their respective flanks as soon as the opposing side players receive the ball.
The whole defense line must move in a compact way, keeping tight and ready to carry out diagonals on side balls and pyramids on those in the center.
When the side defender is contrasting his rival side mid fielder, he must be expecting an overlap made by their side defender. It is, therefore, important for our two players on the flank (side defender and side mid fielder) to work in pairs.
The side mid fielder must first make a quick double up in collaboration with the side defender. When their side defender is overlapping, our two players must be ready to exchange marking.
The side defender who was marking the player in possession

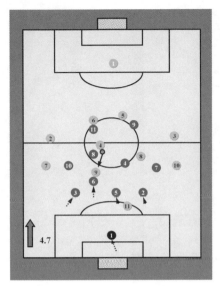

takes the player who is overlapping, while the outside mid fielder who has just been doubling up
takes the player in possession.
The center defenders, on the
other hand, will be watching out
for the so called 'one goes, one
comes' movement made by the
rival strikers in order to create
space.

When one of the two opposing
strikers comes out of our
defense line to meet a mid fielder in possession, our center
defender nearest to him must be
careful not to leave his zone
uncovered. He will have to follow him for a couple of yards and
then let him go. As soon as the striker starts coming back and
enters into our center mid fielder's zone, the center mid fielder
will take him. It is important for our two lines to play very close
together so that the striker we are moving against is handed on
from one line to another without creating gaps in the defense
and without the striker finding himself free of marking. If he
should receive the ball before entering the mid fielders' zone, the
defense must be quick at shortening up on him, leaving the
other striker offside (Fig. 4.7)

We will now have a look at how to keep our opponents from creating a 3 v 2 situation against our center defenders.

In cases where the opponents bring a third player to the central
zone, we must be ready to close him off without finding ourselves
in a dangerous situation of numerical inferiority.

First of all, the line of mid fielders and the line of defenders must
remain close together, with one of the mid fielders closing in on
the opposing player who is creating the momentary situation of
numerical superiority in front of the defense. In particular, the
closing off must be carried out by one of the two mid fielders
making a backward shift. (Fig. 4.8).

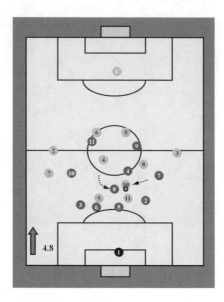

4.8

Should the line of mid fielders find themselves for any reason too far from the opposing player in possession, then, of course, one of our center defenders will have to move out onto him. At this point, the other three defenders will have to tighten in their positions in order to occupy the central space. If possible, when a central defender comes out of the line to close off an opponent, his three section team mates should move up as well towards the ball, leaving the two strikers in an offside position. This in-depth movement on the defenders' part must only take place if there is no other opponent waiting to break in from the back.

Now we must prepare an effective defense movement to contrast an opponent on the flanks in cases where he has created a 3 against 2 in this part of the field.

When our opponents get a center mid fielder to insert himself on the sidelines with their side defender in possession, our side defender must not follow his rival side mid fielder but must wait in the zone. He must close off the center mid fielder who has come to the flank only if, by receiving the ball, this player is in the most advanced position along the sidelines.

As the action develops, if our side defender undergoes overlapping, thus finding himself 1 against 2, he must take on the player who has carried out the overlapping, waiting for his external team mate to close off the player in possession (Fig. 4.9).

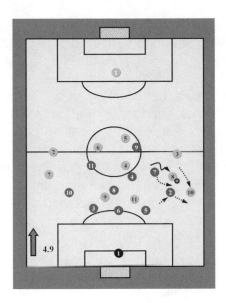

When it is an opposing striker who moves wide, creating numerical superiority along the side and our side defender is putting pressure on the rival side mid fielder, the central defender nearest to this player will have to follow him, with the other three defenders shifting to cover space and the side mid fielder on the other flank integrating himself on the weak side of the defense. Also here, if our side defender who is closing off undergoes an overlapping move, we get the usual exchange of marking with the side mid fielder. As they are shifting to the side where the action is taking place, the other three defenders must be very careful not to leave space in the center and not to be taken by surprise when the rival strikers move into depth.

It is vital in the defense phase to carry out constant and well-organized pressing on your opponents.
In fact, both teams will be in continual pressing on the whole field, and the winner will be whichever of the two has carried this out in the most organized way.
When we lose possession, the whole team must set up the counter-pressing moves that are indispensable if you want to inhibit the ability of the team you are facing.
More than any others, the two center mid fielders will be called on not to give time and space to the two opposing inside mid fielders because, in all likelihood, they will be the ones to set up their team's maneuvers.

In order to create good pressing you must not count your ability to reduce the playing time and space open to the player in possession and to double up on him as often as possible. A fundamental point is that good pressing also comes about as a result of our ability to anticipate our marking on opposing players without the ball, but who, on account of the fact that they are near the player in possession, can receive the ball and bring about a change in play. The player in possession should have the feeling that he is playing 10 against 1: he is being doubled up and there are no free team mates on whom he can dump the ball.

Pressing is based on keeping the team short and tight and maintaining the correct position in reference to the ball in order to block opposing players in support.

Pressing must also be sustained by the constant application of correct offside tactics.

When organizing pressing against a 4-4-2, the coach must prepare the shifting movements with which to press the side defenders.

With a center defender in possession, one of the two strikers closes on him while the other marks the second in anticipation. The line of mid fielders and defenders keep themselves short and compact. The two opposing side defenders are left free so as to invite the player in possession to play the ball on them (Fig. 4.10).

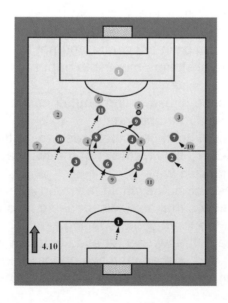

When the ball is going from the center to the side defender, we get a shifting movement on the sidelines. The side mid fielder closes on the side defender and our side defender goes into position as a side mid fielder, taking his team mate's place.
The three defenders shift position, while the far side mid fielder goes back a yard or two, ready to integrate with the defense line and shifting along its weak side should the opposing player in possession manage to play the ball into depth.
The striker who has just been in possession double teams the side defender in possession; and the second striker places himself in such a way as to mark and anticipate the center defender nearest to the ball.
At the same time, the mid fielders shorten in to mark and anticipate the supporting players nearest to the ball. All this is clearly set out in Fig. 4.11.
Comparing Fig. 4.10 and 4.11, you should note the changeover from the stand-by phase to the aggressive phase of pressing, and the fact that the team is attempting to carry out invited pressing.

THE 4-4-2 AGAINST THE 4-3-3

The 4-3-3 is a system usually put into effect by a team that wishes to express spectacular, offensive play.
We should therefore be expecting a very active, aggressive team, which will go into attack with large numbers of players and which puts a wide range of offensive solutions on display.
In the defense phase, such a team will apply ultra-offensive pressing, and the team will be very mobile vertically speaking in order to exploit the offside rule.

Let us now have a look at the numerical situations created by the natural placement of the two teams on the field.
In defense we are in a 4 against 3 situation, in which, even if we have numerical supremacy, we could still meet a lot of problems connected to the many solutions guaranteed by the three-man attacking front.
In the mid field we have numerical superiority once again (4 against 3), while in attack we are 2 against 4.

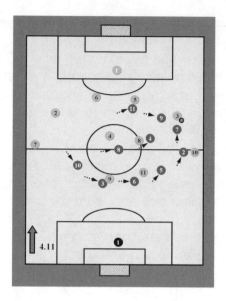

Having made an analysis of the situation section by section, we can now have a look at the field from a vertical point of view. It is not easy to analyze the face off of the two systems along vertical lines because the two opposing center or side mid fielders and the two wings cover hybrid, non-fixed positions.

The fact is that the two side mid fielders are a cross between center mid fielders and real side mid fielders.
In the defense phase they will stay tight, creating a 3 to 2 against our inside mid fielders; in the attacking phase, they will often widen out to collaborate with the wings along the flanks, creating a three-player chain there, which puts our side players in numerical inferiority (3 against 2) on both corridors.
The wings, on the other hand, start off wide, giving our side defenders work to do, and then tighten in to attack space alongside the center forward. As you can see, it is difficult to define the precise placement of these four players because their dynamism can create totally different situations during the course of a single match.

In any case, at the center of our defense we are 2 against 1, while at the center of the attack we are in a favorable 2 against 2 situation.
Fig. 4.12 illustrates the stand off between the two teams on the field.

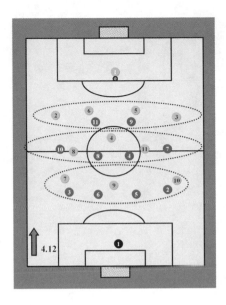 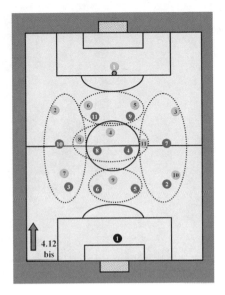

We will now have a more careful look at how to behave during
the various playing phases.

The attacking phase

It is important to make play offensive in the phase of possession
to force our opponents to play in their half. In fact, teams using
the 4-3-3 suffer pressure more than is good for them.
When building up play, the first thing we should try to do is exploit
the 4 against 3 in the mid field.

Note that the three opposing mid fielders will play tight during
their defense phase, and it would, therefore, be a mistake to
channel our play down the center. Quite the opposite, we must
constantly attempt to play out on the side mid fielders who will
have space as a result of the placement of the two teams. They
must position themselves out wide to put the opponent's defense
system under pressure - and they will have difficulty in this part of
the field (Fig. 4.13).

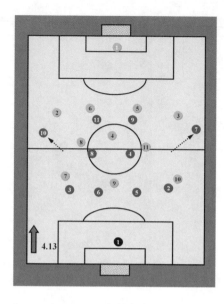

When our side player has received the ball, the opponents will behave in one of two ways as they go in to close us off: either they will bring a side defender into depth or the nearest inside mid fielder will widen out.

In the first case, we will try to exploit the shifting movements of the other three opposing defenders in this way: the nearest strik-

er carries out an in-depth cut from inside to outside, while the other comes to meet the player in possession, allowing him to carry out a vertical pass that is sure to reach its destination.

By giving the ball to a striker who goes into depth you have a good chance of allowing that player to shoot at goal; by passing to the player who has come to meet you, what you get is a change of play towards the other flank (Fig. 4.14).

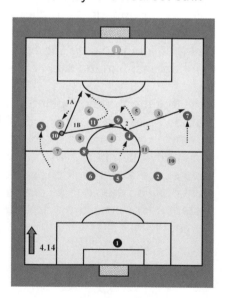

In cases where an opposing inside mid fielder closes in on our side player, there will be a consequent shift on the part of the two rival mid fielders and we should immediately change play to the other side of the field, where there will of course be fewer players. To carry out this change of play you will need the help of at least one striker acting as a wall.

The overlapping moves of the side defenders are very important as well because on the sidelines the opposition can defend with only one player during the defense phase, i.e., the side back. It is therefore necessary to put this player in a 2 v 1 by using the acceleration of our pair of side players.
Note that the opponent's two side mid fielders are not positioned in such a way as to be able to double team our external player. Another weakness of theirs is that they will not be able to shift a fifth player on the weak side of the defense, which will therefore be forced to make fairly long diagonals.
Thus it is important to try to attack the opposition's defense from the blind side, making sudden changes of play which send the ball to the weak side of the field. The blind side of the defense will be attacked by the side mid fielder using a second time cut (Fig. 4.15).
Against the 4-3-3 we must also try to exploit the 2 v 2 that our two strikers have against the opposition's center defenders.

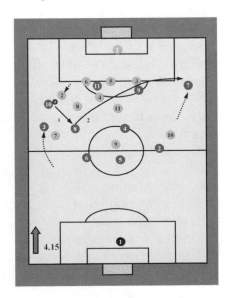

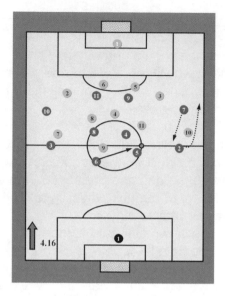

4.16

The side backs can even carry out a 'one comes, one goes' with their relative side mid fielder in order to free space at the side of the defense as well as to increase the dynamics of our play (Fig. 4.16).

With regard to which finishing touch plays we should most frequently put into effect, and keeping in mind that the opponent's defense will be playing very deep - we will have to go into attack using cuts.

Another consideration to be made concerning the 4-3-3 is that in the defense phase this system often changes into a 4-5-1 because the wings shift down to the mid field. Clearly this will only take place in teams with a highly organized defense phase. If our opponents behave in this way, we will have to carry out a movement to get around them to avoid being bottled up in the center. In that case, during finishing touches we will be using crosses as well as cuts.

The last thing to be said about facing a 4-3-3 is that our counter-attack following on positive pressing must be very quick in order to exploit the fact that a team that attacks aggressively will usual-ly disengage their side backs, leaving the two defenders alone in the center. This favorable situation of numerical equality is to be exploited using high speed combinations between the two strik-ers.

It is not a good idea to bring a third player into the central part of the attacking front because the opposing center mid fielder will be playing far back during the defense phase and he gives very good protection to the center defenders, acting as a shield. In connection with the ultra-offensive pressing that our adversaries will be applying, the center defenders will have to be very careful when opening play onto their side backs because the opponent's wings will be putting those players under great pressure.

As a result of this, the center defenders must try to make the most of the 2 v 1 against the opposing center forward, moving in to play the ball onto the side mid fielders, who, as we have already said, have more space open to them (Fig. 4.17). Sending play towards the side mid fielders is, in fact, the best way to get over the opponents' continuous pressing.

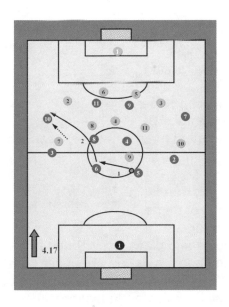

The defense phase

Even in the defense phase, it is very important to make the most of the 4 against 3 situation in the mid field. To do that, our four mid fielders will have to play in such a way as to neutralize the possible numerical inferiority that the two center mid fielders could encounter against the three opposing players in cases where they are playing tight even in the offense phase.

The three opposing mid fielders must be put constantly under pressure so as to exploit our numerical superiority.

It is no good being in numerical superiority in the mid field if you are leaving space and time to your opponents there.

Without considering the characteristics of the particular players interpreting them, the most important roles in the attacking phase of the 4-3-3 are the center mid fielder who is directing operations and the center forward, who, by moving in to meet them, becomes a precise point of reference to his team mates.

We will have to be very careful in wiping out the actions of these two players in particular.

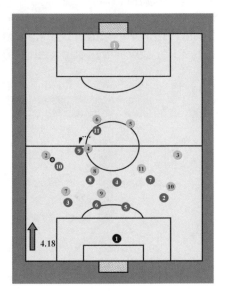

The center mid fielder, who plays a few yards further back than his two section team mates must be put under constant pressure by a center mid fielder coming out of line from the other section team mates, who will then tighten in their positions.

When the line of mid fielders is in pressing against an opposing side mid fielder or a side back who has disengaged himself, one of the two strikers will have to shift backwards to mark and anticipate the center mid fielder (Fig. 4.18).

In certain circumstances it will be one of the two strikers who will directly close in on the opposing center mid fielder as the other two lines shorten up in front.

When, instead, he comes to meet the ball, the opposing center forward must be followed by one of the two center backs, making sure that he cannot turn when he has received it. Here, one of the two center mid fielders must double up to make sure that the center forward cannot dump the ball on a mid fielder who will terminate play.

Two other dangerous players in the 4-3-3's attack are the wings. They will be playing in depth and wide most of the time as points of reference for the other players.

Very often, however, when the center forward comes into depth, freeing space in the center, the two wings cut towards this area creating depth and going in to make the most of the space that is opening up.

This will allow the player in possession to carry out a vertical pass that will be very dangerous for our defense.

Even when one of the two wings is in possession along the sidelines, the other will make a cut in towards our goal, going with the center forward.

From the point of view of our defenders, the wings' cuts towards the interior will be made principally between the side and the center backs.

It is important to try to stop the wings from making these in-depth cuts, but when it happens, our defenders will have to behave in such a way as to make sure that these forward movements do not permit the opponent to shoot at goal.

By pressing the opposing mid fielders and side defenders you force the wings to move back in order to give support to their team mates in difficulty. In that way you prevent them from moving into depth, and, when one of them has received the ball he will easily be doubled by our outside mid fielder (Fig. 4.19). The wings can carry out three main cuts:

☐ Cut to enter between the side back and the center defender;
☐ Cut to enter behind the side back;
☐ Cut to receive a ball above the defense line.

When a wing makes a cut between the side and center back, the latter must try to anticipate, placing himself on the line of the pass, while the side back must continue following the opponent in order to close in on him when and if he receives the ball (Fig. 4.20). In order to absorb the wing's cut in as well as possible, the

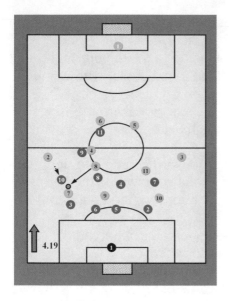

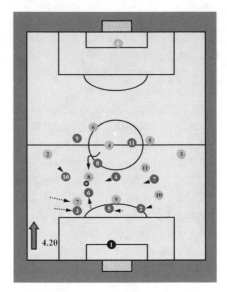

center defender must try to put his body between his opponent and the goal.

If the wing cuts in behind our side back, the defense, which is already in line, will behave in one of two ways, depending on the wing's starting position. If the wing sets off level with our defense line, we must move up a yard or two to put him in an offside position. If the wing starts his move from behind the defense line, we must move back quickly to absorb the in-depth movement, reducing the area behind us.

In cases where the wing cuts in to receive the ball above our defense line, the side back and the center defender must exchange marking with perfect timing (Fig. 4.21).

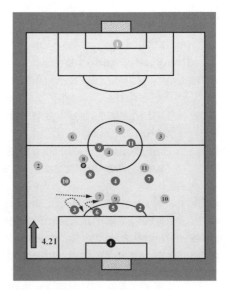

Another movement that the opposing three-man attacking front will often carry out is a give and follow combination between the wing and the center forward.

When the wing - closed off by the side back - passes the ball to the center forward who is being followed by the center defender, and then, instead of going into depth, sprints horizontally parallel with our defense line, it must be our other center defender who closes him off. Clearly, the nearest side back and the other center defender must cover him on each side (defense pyramid), while the side back who was originally contrasting the wing will tighten his position. The side back on the opposite flank from the one where the play began must be ready to absorb the other wing's cut in, which is a typical movement coming after the give and follow that has just taken place.

The vital thing is to get control of the players making up the opponent's three-man attacking front because these are the real points of reference for our opponent's moves.

In fact, the most notable thing about the 4-3-3 is their constant attempts to send the ball vertically to the attacking players; if you want to stop them, then basically you are going to have to close them off and double up.

Another important thing against a 4-3-3 is to know how to face the 3 against 2 situation along the sidelines. When their left back is moving with the ball, our side player must close him off. The wing moving to meet his team mates must be followed by the side back, while their center mid fielder moving towards the sides must be followed by our nearest center mid fielder.

In all plays along the sidelines involving three opponents, our nearest center mid fielder must help his team mates on the corresponding flank.

One last consideration to be made about the defense phase of the 4-3-3 is that in the attacking phase this system will often set up a five-man mid field, because the two side backs move into depth together alongside the three basic mid fielders.

In order to deal with this possible numerical inferiority in the mid field, our four players of the section must be playing tight, ready at all times to make diagonal cuts on the opposing side backs should they receive the ball.

As soon as we regain possession we must immediately send the ball vertically to the strikers who will now be in a favorable 2 to 2 situation against the opposition's center defenders.

THE 4-4-2 AGAINST THE 3-4-3

The 3-4-3 system gives better defense coverage than the 4-3-3, while in attack it guarantees a range of solutions very near to our own. All this in spite of the deceptive appearance of the system. In fact, the back line hardly ever persists as a three-man defense system during the phase of non-possession, but, as a result of the side mid fielders' shifts to the flank of the defense, it turns itself into a four or even a five-man section depending on where the ball is.

If the team is well organized, during the phase of non-possession, the two wings also shift back into the mid field, taking the places left vacant when the side mid fielders moved down to the defense. In the defense phase, therefore, the system changes itself into a 5-4-1, in which the defense line is full of players and well-covered in the center. In fact the original three defenders tighten up their positions trying to fill the central spaces, while the flanks are guarded by the two side mid fielders.

So the 3-4-3 can have different faces in the defense phase depending on the position of the ball.

When one of our defenders is in possession, the placement of the opposing team remains the same; with one of our side mid fielders in possession their system becomes a 4-4-2 because of the shifts carried out on the weak side by their side mid fielder and their wing, who go to join the defense and the mid field respectively; with one of our center mid fielders or strikers in possession the other system becomes a 5-4-1. The opposition's coach could also decide to keep to his team's original placement when one of our center mid fielders is in possession because their three defenders are in numerical superiority over our strikers. In that case, however, their defense line would not be able to guarantee the best coverage of the different parts of the field, which can only take place using a 4 or 5-man defense. We will see later how to make the best of this weakness in a three-man defense.

In the attacking phase, on the other hand, the 3-4-3 can make use of three players on each flank: the side backs, the side mid fielders and the wings. Also, this system enjoys the verve that comes from having a three-man attacking front.

Let us now have a look at the numerical situation section by section.
As we can see in Fig. 4.22, in defense we find ourselves 4 against 3; in the mid field there is numerical equality, 4 against 4; and in attack our two strikers are facing three rival defenders.

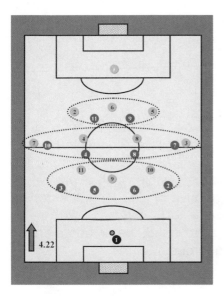 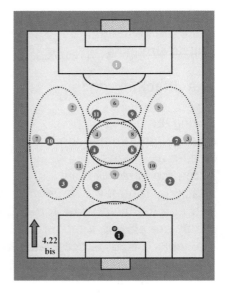

As for the situation on the flanks, we must distinguish cases where we are in the attacking phase from cases where we are in the phase of non-possession. In the first, we will find ourselves in a 2 against 2 situation along the flanks if their wing is collaborating actively with his team mates in the defense phase. If he is not doing so we could even be in a favorable 2 to 1 situation against the opposition's side mid fielder.
When we are in the defense phase, we get a 3 against 2 set up in our opponent's favor.

In the center of the field our two inside mid fielders are in numerical equality against the two opposing center mid fielders; in the center of the defense, our pair of center backs is in numerical superiority against the rival center forward, even if they will have to be on the alert for the wings' movements.

As far as the situation in the center of the attack is concerned, we have to make a distinction here as well, depending on the phase of play.

In the possession phase, and given their three defenders playing tight, our two strikers are in numerical inferiority (2 against 3); in the phase of non-possession, on account of the side backs widening out, our two strikers will find themselves in front of a single center defender.

Let us now have a look at how to behave in both phases so as to make the best of the 3-4-3's weaknesses and at the same time limit its strengths.

The attacking phase

During the attacking phase we will have to turn our attention to how we are to make the best of the weaknesses connected to a three-man defense.

Three men are not sufficient to cover the whole width of our attacking front. If the three members have to play wide, the gaps between them would be too extended.

If they are playing too tight, on the other hand, the corridors on the flanks would be completely unguarded.

We must play in such a way as to:

❑ Stretch out the opposing defense to make the best use of the wide open spaces in the center.

❑ Exploit the space on the flanks.
   It goes without saying that we must vary the solution time after time.

The work of the two strikers is important in widening out the defense. With a mid fielder in possession, they must make a simultaneous movement towards the opposite sidelines. The two defenders will widen out to go after them and you will get open space in the middle of the attacking front.

These spaces must immediately be attacked by the side mid fielders breaking into the center.

The player in possession will be able to pass to one of them directly (Fig. 4.23) or he can give the ball to one of the strikers who has just widened out, and play a one/two into open space.

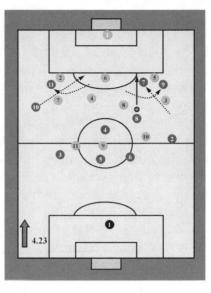

The second play is connected with making the best use of the space left unguarded on the sidelines.

It is obviously the two side mid fielders who should carry out the right movements.

With one of the center mid fielders in possession, the two strik-

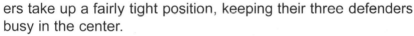

ers take up a fairly tight position, keeping their three defenders busy in the center.

At the same time, the two side mid fielders sprint into the free spaces along the sidelines. One of the two will be given the ball by the player in possession, either directly or using a dump and rebound pass with the help of a striker.

The two opposing side mid fielders will be attracted towards the flanks to intercept our two players who are breaking in. As a result, their mid field will now comprise only two players: the two

internal mid fielders. Our two side backs must immediately insert themselves alongside the center mid fielders. In this way, should there be any difficulty opening up play on the side mid fielders breaking into depth along the flanks, our player in possession will be able to pass the ball to one of the side defenders who have just come up and are free of marking. This movement is shown in Fig. 4.24.

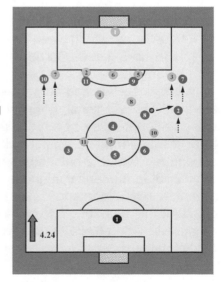

If the opponent should turn out to be particularly dangerous in the attacking phase, we could use the following technique in order to force them to defend with so many men that they will not be able to create problems even if they regain possession. This move consists in having our two side mid fielders play constantly deep to force the two opposing side mid fielders to move back in order not to leave the defense 3 against 4.

Our two side backs will come alongside the two center mid fielders, recreating the four-man mid field. At this point, we force the opponent's two wings to shift back to the mid field so as not to be in a 2 against 4 situation there. Now the layout of the two teams has been changed completely: from a 4-4-2 against a 3-4-3 to a 2-4-4 against a 5-4-1. There is no risk in leaving the two center defenders alone because during a counter attack they will be in a 2 to 1 situation against the single opposing striker.

Even though the opponents now have a nine-man defense, they will still be having problems in this situation, for the two wings cannot provide adequate defense coverage, and, in any case, an opponent lined up with a 3-4-3 is certainly not prepared to carry out a defensive match.

One thing is sure: in such a tactical situation, we will need to play on the sidelines, getting our side defenders to set up play.

Whatever the situation, we must always direct our play onto the flanks, both when the two wings are participating in the defense phase and in cases where the flanks are guarded only by the opposing side mid fielders. This is necessary because the spaces in the center are clogged up by the presence of the two rival center mid fielders and the three central defenders.

In cases where we find ourselves in a favorable situation along the sidelines (2 against 1) it is important to make the best of it using adequate play by our two pairs of side players. The side back must overlap continually with the side mid fielder when the second receives the ball. In that way the opponent's side player will be put in numerical inferiority.

The side mid fielder, and consequently the whole opposing team could, at this point begin to behave in different ways. Depending on how they do so, we will ourselves come up with different playing solutions.

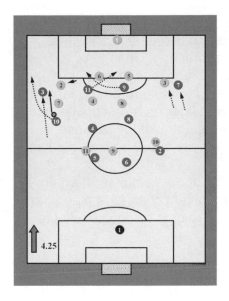

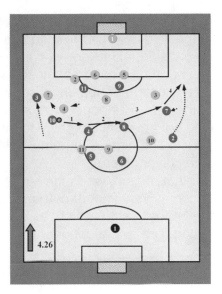

If the opposing side mid fielder continues to mark our player in possession, he will have to give the ball to the overlapping side mid fielder forcing the opponent's defense to shift. As the three opposing defenders are making this shift to go and close on our side defender, the strikers will move into depth to take advantage of the space that has just been created. The side mid fielder who has just furnished the side back with the ball, will now overlap in his turn creating further difficulties for the opposition's defense system (Fig. 4.25).

On the contrary, if the side defender moves back to mark our side defender breaking in, our side mid fielder in possession will now be free and with space in front. He will try to make the best of that space, moving up with the ball and closing in on the opponent's goal, waiting for another opponent to close on him. If a center defender comes out to do so, the two strikers must move into depth making a crossover to create even more problems for the defense, which is already in difficulty. If it is a center mid fielder who moves back to close him off, then our player in possession must make a change of play onto the flank on the far side, which will not be covered on account of the shift made by the entire defense line onto the strong side of the field (Fig. 4.26).

Another case in which play should be changed onto the far side of the field is when the wing has time to move back and close in on our side mid fielder who is free of marking. Change of play is an important weapon against the 3-4-3 because there will always be a situation of numerical superiority in our favor on the far side of the field. The opponent's side mid fielder on the opposite side, who will have shifted down to the weak flank of the defense, is sure to find himself in numerical inferiority 1 to 2 against our two side players there.

For that reason, when the strong part of the field is blocked up, it becomes very important to make an instant change of play onto the opposite side, which, as we have said, is being actively protected by a single opponent.

How should the two strikers behave in order to get past the three man defense? They must be able to exchange passes so as to jump the opposition.

When a mid fielder is in possession they can do the following:

☐ Make crossovers, carrying out inverted cuts between the respective center defenders and the sweeper.

☐ One of the two widens out towards the sidelines followed by a center defender; when he receives the ball, the other striker makes a cut in the direction of the goal and then converges towards his team mate.

In this way the center defender on the far side is cut out of play, and the sweeper, because he is being attacked in depth, risks not being able to get back on top. The striker who has made the movement in deviation must immediately rebound on the striker who is cutting in. As we can see in Fig. 4.27, our striker receives the ball in depth while the entire opposing defense has been cut out of play.

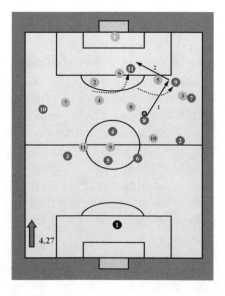

4.27

182

As regards the management of the ball in the defense section, what we said concerning the 4-3-3 holds here as well. We must be careful about the fact that our side defenders are being marked and pressed by the opponent's wings. We must begin play in the center, making the best use of our center defenders' 2 to 1 situation against the rival center forward. In this case as well, the side backs can make 'one goes, one comes' movements with the side mid fielders in an attempt to 'get rid of' the two opposing wings freeing space at the side of the two center defenders.
In any case, when the two defenders are moving with the ball in the center, the two inside mid fielders must come to meet them in support to create safe points of reference for their team mates from the third line. In order to get around our adversary's ultra-offensive pressing, it is important that all four mid fielders are placed correctly so as to form those tiers and ranks that will result in the triangles and rhombus shapes so necessary to make sure the ball can move ahead in a safe and linear way.
When they are being pressed, the four defenders must make sure the ball never goes in a direction parallel with the mid field line. The four members of the defense line must place themselves in a crescent shape with the two center players in line: this will make it more difficult for the opponents to intercept the ball. When one of the center defenders is in possession, the other must move back - to give him support, but also so that he can intervene should the opponent manage to steal the ball.

The finishing touch technique to be most frequently used in order to arrive at a position where you can take a shot is the cross from the sidelines or a dump made by one striker on the other or a pass made by a striker on a crossover movement when the mid fielder who receives the pass is breaking into the space created by the striker.

The defense phase

Even against a 3-4-3 it is important to limit the movements of the three rival strikers. Even though we are in numerical superiority in defense (4 against 3), we will find it difficult to manage the three-man attacking front, which guarantees our opponents a great number of offensive solutions. Also, the three opposing strikers

are an important point of reference for their team mates in the
sections behind them. Above all
the three defenders will often be
relying on the corresponding
strikers coming to meet them in
order to bring the ball into depth.
One of the strong points of the 3-
4-3 is that it makes it easy for
the team to draw up the rhombus
shapes so necessary to move
the ball forward with perfect
geometry. The attacking player
coming to meet his respective
defender can, having received
the ball with his back to the goal,

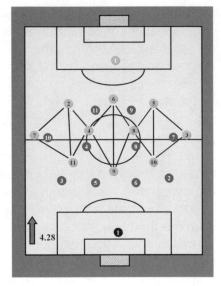

then dump it with great confidence on one of the nearby mid
fielders. It is the placement of the 3-4-3 that creates this perfect
natural grouping of the players (Fig. 4.28).

It follows that we must cancel out the players making up the
three man attack, in order to put a stop to the opposing team's
ability to bring the ball forward building up play in a dangerous
way.
We must also say that the 3-4-3's attacking front will generally
tend to play more tightly than that of the 4-3-3. This comes about
because the three strikers of the 3-4-3 do not have to worry so
much about covering the whole width of the attacking front, in
that the two side mid fielders, who will be playing in depth during
the offense phase, do a very good job of looking after that particular problem.
The result is that all three strikers might be playing very near our
two center defenders, keeping them dangerously under pressure.
Against this kind of problem, the side backs must keep themselves fairly tight to make sure they can 'contain' the three man
attacking front.
When an attacking player goes to meet his respective defender
(the right wing goes to meet the right side defender, the center
forward goes to meet a center defender or the left wing goes up
to the left side back) or a mid fielder, our nearest defender must
follow him to put him under immediate pressure, not letting him

turn round. When the attacking player has received the ball, our mid fielder must double team him straight away to stop him from dumping the ball behind.

The moment our defender comes out of the defense line to follow an attacking player going to meet his team mate, the other three members of the defense must tighten in their positions in order not to leave dangerous space that can be attacked by the opponents breaking in from behind. When the attacking player - closed in on by our defender - receives the ball with his back to the goal, the other three members of the defense line must immediately shorten in towards the ball to increase the pressure, exploiting the fact that the opponent cannot play it forward. If the defense elastic is being applied correctly, the other attacking players will be left offside, which will at the same time only increase our chances of regaining possession at once on account of the hard pressing we are putting on the player in possession. Even against the three man attack of the 3-4-3 we must know how to face the various types of cutting movements that the wings will be carrying out. Concerning these, we can refer back to what was said about the three man attacking front of the 4-3-3. There is also a particular play often used by a team adopting the 3-4-3, which we should keep in mind to prepare ourselves as well as possible if it is carried out during a match.

The play goes like this: with a side defender in possession, the side mid fielder widens out, keeping the sideline to his back while the wing comes to meet him.

Suddenly the wing cuts in towards the center in the space between our defense and the mid field. At the same time the other two attacking players 'wheel round' to allow the wing who has called the movement to take up position as side attacking player opposite the ball. One of the two attacking players can therefore rebound on the wing who is cutting horizontally across the field. At the same time as the wing's movement, the side mid

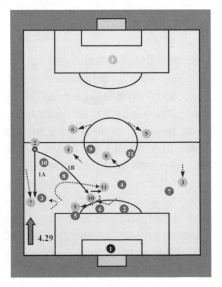

4.29

fielder sprints into depth, exploiting the free space on the flank. In order to grasp this movement you can refer to Fig. 4.29.

Using this play, our opponents can make the best of the flank by creating and attacking the space resulting from the collaboration between the side mid fielder and the wing. In addition, the wheeling movement of the three strikers can create serious problems for our four defenders.

To make sure that our opponents do not become too dangerous, it is important, first of all, that our side back following the wing initially is ready to move back to his original position the moment the wing suddenly changes direction. In this way, the side mid fielder breaking down the flanks will not find free space. What to do about the wheeling movement of the three strikers? Our four defenders must keep their heads and stay where they are. The wing cutting in above the defense moving away from the ball should be left momentarily free of marking. In fact, the other side defender should wait for him in his zone. If one of the two attacking players who have shifted their positions towards the ball manages to rebound onto the wing as he is cutting in, the defender that happens to occupy the zone in which the ball is passing must come out in contrast on the new player in possession, while the other three team mates create the necessary cover with diagonals and pyramids.

Against the 3-4-3 it is also important to know how to face the overlapping carried out by the side mid fielder when the wing is in possession. The side mid fielder / wing overlapping moves of the 3-4-3 are similar to ones carried out by the side defender and side mid fielder of the 4-4-2, and so what we said there is valid here as well. The side defender marking the wing should let him go, taking on the side mid fielder as he is overlapping. The wing will remain free for a moment or two in the meantime, but he must be closed off as quickly as possible by our side mid fielder who moves back to assist his side team mate.

The overlapping move between the side mid fielder and the wing will probably take place near the penalty area, with the risk that, in those few moments that the wing is left free of marking, he will create serious problems by crossing or even shooting at goal. To make sure that does not happen, our pairs of side players on both flanks must play very close together so that our side mid fielder can close in as fast as possible on the wing in possession. The fact that the side back and the side mid fielder are playing close together is important, apart from any considerations connected with the opposing side mid fielder's overlapping plays. The side attacking player is usually gifted with technical ability that allows him to dribble past his opponent. It is important, therefore, that he should not be allowed to face our side back 1 against 1.

The 3-4-3 system will usually exploit the sidelines to arrive at the finishing touch phase by crosses from the base line. The center forward is often a player who is very good in the air.

Crosses into the penalty area could therefore be fatal to us.

For this reason it is very important to close off as well as possible all the spaces open to our opponents on the sidelines by the correct placement of our pairs of side players when the ball is on the flank. Our opponent's side players must be pressed and we must double up on them continually. In particular, when, after having received the ball, the rival side player is closed off by our side mid fielder, our inside mid fielder must immediately go and double up on the marking. The side back must never go to help the side mid fielder by doubling up with him in front because that would leave the defense 3 against 3 with the nearest wing having space and freedom. Against the 3-4-3 it is important to make the most of the difficulty this system creates during positive transition. When a team using the 3-4-3 regains possession, their players will have difficulty passing from the positions of the defense phase which has just concluded to those of the attacking phase which is just about to begin. The side mid fielders will find themselves very far back on a level with the defense and they need time to get back into the right position on the sidelines. Also the members of the defense need time to get from their tight positions in the non-possession phase to their widened out places in the phase of possession.

We will have to exploit our opponent's difficulty to move from their positions in the defense phase to those of the attacking phase. Here, our pressing on the rival defenders and mid fielders must be immediate so as not to give the side mid fielders time to move up and the two side backs to widen out.

The opposing player in possession will be forced, therefore, to carry out a long pass, which, apart from lengthening out the team, will probably have to be met by a single striker, because the two wings will probably still find themselves behind beside the inside mid fielders.

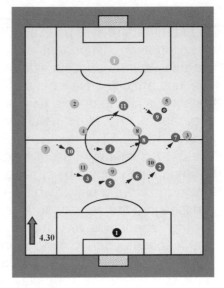

We must program the pressing that our team will have to effect on the three opposing defenders. The two strikers must always press the opposing side backs, even when they are playing wide on the flanks.

In this way, we wipe out the opponent's possible numerical superiority (3 to 2) on each flank.

The right striker should pressing the left side back, while the left striker presses the right side defender.

When one of the strikers is pressing a side back, the other striker must place himself on the sweeper's passing lines to carry out anticipatory marking (Fig. 4.30).

When the sweeper is in possession, the two strikers can place themselves in two different ways:

☐   Axial placement (Fig. 4.31). One of the two strikers goes to press the sweeper and the other places himself in a vertical position a yard or two behind, ready to close off the side back receiving the ball from the sweeper.

☐   In-line placement. The two strikers position themselves each in the space separating the nearest side back and the sweeper, trying to cover the passing lines. The sweeper is left momentarily free of marking, but the moment he advances too far both strikers should go in to close him off immediately.

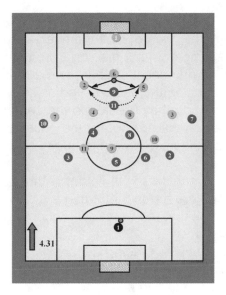

The first of these two set ups is the better in cases where the three defenders are playing close together, the second in the opposite conditions. This comes about because if we use axial marking against a three man defense playing wide the striker would not be able to close off the two side backs when his opponent received the ball because he would be too far away.

It is better not to send the side mid fielders to close off the side backs because a shift along the side lines would be useless if not actually dangerous. It is much more convenient, as we have said above, to widen out the strikers in pressing to affront the groups of three players on each flank (side back, side mid fielder, wing).

THE 4-4-2 AGAINST THE 3-4-1-2

The 3-4-1-2 has been the system most commonly used in Italy in the last few years, even if there has been a recent return to the 4-4-2. The first thing we must say is that the 3-4-1-2 was born to create problems for the 4-4-2. The presence of the attacking mid fielder floating between the lines of the opponent's defense and mid field puts the defense system of the 4-4-2 in serious difficulty because they have to control a player who is very dynamic and whose position is not fixed but, on the contrary, extremely variable. You could even call most of these players 'all fielders' because they are always moving around a good part of the whole playing area. In fact, they do not limit themselves to the three quarters of the attacking front but also go to regain possession in the mid field, creating numerical superiority there; they give depth on the sidelines by placing themselves vertically to the side mid fielder in possession; and they break into the center of the attack, creating a three man offensive front for the occasion and working with the normal two strikers to create serious problems for the rival defense line.

If the presence of the attacking mid fielder is the 3-4-1-2's strong point, its weaknesses are the fact that there is only one player on each flank and the risk that the team can become over-depend- ent on its 'creative' player.

It will be clear then that when facing a team organized in this way we must try to exploit these weaknesses while at the same time managing as well as we can to keep the attacking mid fielder in hand.

Let us now have a look at the numerical counter position of the two teams on the field by setting out the situation section by sec- tion.

In defense we have a 4 against 2, keeping in mind, however, that when the attacking mid fielder breaks into the attack the situation will be 4 against 3, in which our opponents can be dangerous if our defense section is caught unawares.

In the mid field we have numerical equality 4 against 4, but even here our mid fielders must be ready for a situation of inferiority created by the attacking mid fielder when he moves back to receive the ball from the mid fielders.

In attack we are 2 to 3 against the opposing trio of defenders. You must remember, however, that even with the 3-4-1-2 there will be shifting moves that will vary the entire set up of the sys- tem. When the ball is in the center, the two side mid fielders slip back alongside the defense; with the ball on the sidelines, the side mid fielder on the strong side stays in depth to 'press' the ball while the opposite side mid fielder integrates with the defense (all of whose members have in the meantime shifted towards the flank with the ball) shifting onto the weak side.

In the phase of non-possession the attacking mid fielder will probably shift to the center, and this will create a 5-3-2 with a ball in the middle and a 4-4-2 with the ball at the side.

Making an analysis of the tactical situation in the various parts of the field, we can see that we are in numerical superiority on each flank (2 against 1); at the center of the field we are 2 against 2; while in attack our two strikers have to get over the opposition of the three opposing defenders. The attacking mid fielder can modify the numerical situation in different parts of the field: in the attacking phase he can establish numerical equality on the flank where the ball is being played, so keeping our side back under pressure; he can create numerical superiority in attack (3 against 2) by breaking into the center; and lastly he can put our two center mid fielders in numerical inferiority (2 against 3) by moving back to the mid field. We must also add that, as opposed to the 3-4-3, the two side backs should not create problems for us in the defense phase. In any case, as we will see when we are treating the defense phase, the strikers will be looking after them.

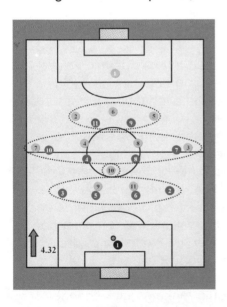
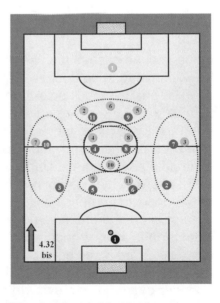

We can see how the two line ups differ in Fig. 4.32. However, as we have already said, the dynamism of the attacking mid fielder and the continual vertical movements of the two side mid fielders to cover the whole flank will lead to the creation of situations on the field that are completely different from the 3-4-1-2's original set up as laid out in the diagram.

We will now have a look at the behavior to adopt in both phases.

The attacking phase

The first thing we must do in the attacking phase is to make the best of the fact that the 4-4-2 gives us a pair of players on each flank, while the 3-4-1-2 has only one along the sides. In order to exploit this favorable numerical superiority we will have to try to direct play constantly to the flanks.

The ball can be passed to the side back or the side mid fielder, and in each case play will develop differently.
If the side back receives the ball, he will have to move with it, obliging the opposing side mid fielder to shift on him. At the same time, our side mid fielder sprints into depth, putting the opponent's three defenders in difficulty - they will have to shift on him to resolve their side back's situation of numerical inferiority.
During this shift that the defenders are forced to carry out without the ball being in movement, our strikers can find open spaces to attack by moving into depth.

In the second case, if the ball is passed to our side mid fielder, he will have to bring it forward closed in on by their side mid fielder while our side back quickly makes an overlapping move on the outside to put the opposing side player in a 1 against 2 situation. We must try to make the best of overlapping moves, whether the side back is taken on by the opposing side mid fielder who was contrasting our side mid fielder (and that will create space for the latter, allowing him to continue moving up with the ball at his feet) or the opposing defense shifts down to close off our side defender (and, as in the preceding case, that will involve a moment of indecision in the opponent's defense, to be exploited by the strikers' cuts or the insertion of a center mid fielder).
We must also remember that if we obtain no particular benefit from our overlapping move, we should make a quick change of play in order to take our opponents by surprise on the blind side. This can be done in cases where, in spite of their initial situation of numerical inferiority, the opposition have managed to close off all the gaps on the sideline by making a perfect lateral shift along the whole defense line, or by bringing back an attacking player to close us off, or by widening a center mid fielder onto the flank. Apart from considerations such as these, against the 3-4-1-2 you

can always profit by making a change of play because you are sure to be in numerical superiority (2 against 1) on the far side of the field, and so these continuous overlapping moves between the two side players will be all the more dangerous for your opponent. They will have great difficulty resolving the problem of their numerical inferiority on the weak side because all of their players will be positioned on the part of the field where the ball was in play before the change took place (Fig. 4.33).

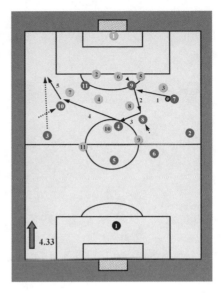

In opening up play, it is always better for our center mid fielders to pass the ball to the more advanced side player because the numerical superiority is easier to exploit by having the side back make the overlapping move. In any case, when our center mid fielder is in possession, the nearest pair of side players should move up to give him the chance to make an easy and convenient pass either to the side back or to the side mid fielder. Also, the two players on each flank must stay together in order to make the most of their collaboration in exploiting the numerical superiority along the sidelines.

The center defenders should always set off play by sending the ball to the side defenders, forcing the opposing team to shift along the external lines. Ideally, as far as we are concerned at least, this shift should take place when the ball is not in transmission. That would be very dangerous for our opponents, because, as we have already said, we will be able to use free space or free men during the shifting move. In addition, the side backs will have space to use, and this would be a sure outlet to get around the opposing strikers' pressing on our center defenders.

The two pairs of side players can make other alternative movements to those we have already seen. Here are a couple examples:

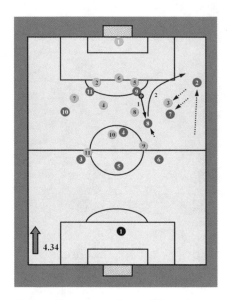 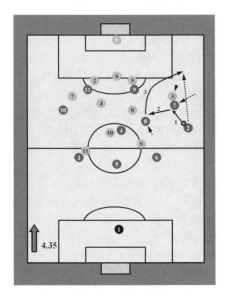

Interchange of position between a side back and a side mid fielder (Fig. 4.34).

With the ball in possession of a center mid fielder, a side mid fielder creates space for the disengagement of the side defender by coming to meet the player in possession or by moving back in a vertical direction.

The opposing side mid fielder is brought away by our side mid fielder's movements and the side back breaks in along the flank, sprinting into depth.

Indirect overlapping by the side defender (Fig. 4.35).

With a side defender in possession, instead of sprinting into depth, the side mid fielder comes to meet his team mate on the flank, bringing his marker with him. The side defender passes the ball to the side mid fielder who is moving back.

As the side back is overlapping his team mate now in possession, the nearest center mid fielder tightens in and moves back to support the man with the ball. This player dumps the ball on the player who has come in support who rebounds at once on the side defender who is now in the wing position. He will receive the ball undisturbed because the only opponent on the sidelines has been brought away by our side mid fielder. An opposing defender will have to close on our player in possession, forcing the other two into a dangerous shift. Once again, the strikers can make the best of this situation by attacking the spaces as they are moving into depth. Our other side mid fielder's insertion on the blind side will create more problems for the opposition. If the opponent's defense is well placed at the moment in which the side defender receives the ball from the center mid fielder, it is better that one of the two strikers comes to meet our player in possession so he can make a give and go pass to arrive at a cross from the base line.

Inside cut by the side mid fielder and disengagement of the side back (Fig. 4.36).
With a center defender or mid fielder in possession, the side mid fielder cuts in towards the center, bringing the opposing side mid fielder away from the flank with him. The side back immediately breaks into depth along the space created on the flank, receiving the ball as he runs. During this combined movement made by the pair of side players to free themselves of marking, the strikers must move together to get away from their own marking. One of the strikers, in particular, comes to meet and support the player in possession who has set up the movement - and he will act as a rebound for the side mid fielder cutting in or for the side back going into depth, so giving the player in possession another

passing option. If he does not receive the ball, the striker who went originally into depth must now change direction to meet the new player in possession, setting up the chance of a triangular exchange, while the striker who had gone to meet the ball must now go into depth, waiting for a pass from his team mate in possession. Clearly, the first player in possession should pass the ball to the disengaged side back either directly or by a dump and rebound on the striker.

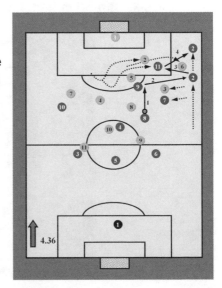

Having now made a detailed examination of the advantages of play along the sidelines, we will move on to look at two other favorable plays that we can use to exploit the weaknesses of the 3-4-1-2 in defense. Both of these make the best of the fact that three defenders are not enough to cover the whole width of the field.

In the first case, we can widen out the three defenders in order to create gaps between them to be attacked, getting the mid fielders to break in from behind. If one of our mid fielders or a side defender is in possession and the opposing side mid fielders have not yet shifted to the sides of the three man defense, our two strikers must deviate and widen themselves out as much as possible to force the three opposing defenders to do the same in order to control them. One or two of our mid fielders must break in rapidly to make the best of the space created - receiving the ball as they do so. Fig. 4.23 shows this movement.
The following is the play to make most use of when the side defender is in possession. The side mid fielder widens out to the sideline, turning his back to it. A moment later the striker also goes towards the flank, attracting the center defender in order to create space in the middle. As the ball is rolling towards the strik-er now placed vertically to him, the side mid fielder cuts in to the center, making for the space created by the striker. The striker will then make a crossed rebound on his team mate breaking in. The play is illustrated in Fig. 4.37.

Another play aiming to exploit the weaknesses of the three man defense is to keep our side mid fielders constantly in depth, practically alongside our strikers. The opponent's side mid fielders will then be forced to remain permanently on a level with the defense, and the two center mid fielders will be left alone. By playing in this way, we lower our opponent's point of balance. Above all the two side mid fielders will be forced to remain too much on the defensive.

At this point, with our two side backs moving up beside the pair of center mid fielders, we will have conspicuous numerical superiority in the mid field (4 against 2). We will easily be able to bring the ball in front of the opponent's defense.

Another thing: the opponent will be forced to bring their attacking mid fielder back to the level of the two center mid fielders in order to oppose this crushing numerical inferiority there, and this will have the effect of reducing the danger he represents should our team lose possession. The only problem this will create for us is that our two center defenders will be forced to play in 'pure system' against their two strikers (2 to 2). However, as we are compressing our opponents around their penalty area, it will not be easy for them to counterattack and pass the ball in any effective way to the strikers, who will also be undergoing immediate pressing.

Apart from creating space for the secondary insertion of the mid fielders, the strikers will have to try to carry out dump and rebound passes on each other to jump the three man defense with a couple of exchanges. For this we refer you back to what we said about the 3-4-3 (c.f. Fig. 4.27).

How to get over our opponent's pressing? As we have already said, the center defenders should constantly send play to the side backs, who will have more freedom.

In fact, we must always open play onto the sidelines, not only because of our numerical superiority in this part of the field, but also because, on account of the attacking mid fielder's integration with the two center mid fielders in this part of the field, we would risk finding ourselves 3 against 2 there, in our opponent's favor.

We should add that, instead of integrating himself with the mid field during the defense phase, the attacking mid fielder sometimes goes to help the strikers in their ultra-offensive pressing. In particular, he will press the center of their defense, while the strikers widen out to put their rival side defenders under pressure. This happens when the 3-4-1-2 is facing a three-man defense. As we have four defenders, the attacking mid fielder will probably not help the strikers with their pressing, but is more likely to shift onto his own mid field line.

To conclude, we can say that the finishing touch techniques most widely used must be crosses from the base line and penetration from the center by making dump and rebound passes in favor of the mid fielders breaking into the lines.

Defense phase

Our greatest worry during the defense phase is the opponent's attacking mid fielder. He is the source of all the opposition's moves because the team will be relying on him when building up play.

By moving between our two lines, the attacking mid fielder will be giving us a lot of purely tactical problems when we are forced to defend ourselves in our own half.
The first thing to say is that our defense and mid field lines must place themselves close to each other to diminish the space in which the attacking mid fielder is free to 'float'. Playing very short is vital in reducing the chances that the opposition's 'creative' player has to make any plays that might turn out decisive.

How to manage a player like this? Marking him man-to-man is not a good idea for two main reasons: first of all, the best way to control an opponent is through collective (or zonal) rather than individual marking. 'Collective marking' gives us the advantage, in practice, of making sure that two players are marking one: our player in the zone where the opponent happens to be is marking him in anticipation, while the other player is ready to close up in cases where the pass is not intercepted. The team must always move in a compact way in response to the ball; no one must ever move after the man.
Marking the attacking mid fielder will depend essentially on the position he takes up in relation to the ball. We will have a look at what our players should do depending on the zone occupied by the attacking mid fielder.

If he keeps to his original position on our three quarters, he must be marked by a mid fielder moving back or a defender coming out of his line - that will depend on how near he is to one or the other. If he is nearer to our back line a nearby defender will come out on him, whereas if he is nearer to the half way line he will be taken by the mid fielder nearest to him, who will move back a yard or two from the line of the other three mid fielders.
The center mid fielder nearest to the attacking mid fielder must mark him in anticipation to put him in the 'shadow zone', and he must carry out diagonals on side balls along with the whole mid field line. The distance between our nearest mid fielder and the opponent's attacking mid fielder will depend on how far he is from the ball. It is all a question of anticipating: the nearer the attacking mid fielder is to the ball the closer our mid fielder in the zone should stay on him; the further away he is, the greater the anticipatory distance the mid fielder in his zone will give him.

As we have already said, however, when the attacking mid fielder moves back to receive the ball from the mid fielders he will put our mid field line in numerical inferiority - from a 4 against 4 we will now be standing up to a 4 against 5 in our opponent's favor. With the ball along the sidelines the problem is reduced. The mid field line shifts towards the ball, tightening up the spaces on the strong side, while the side mid fielder across the field is now completely free. One of the two strikers will have to move back a yard or two, putting himself on the passing lines of an opposing inside mid fielder to facilitate the work of our strikers. On a side ball, of course, the other striker should cover a back pass that a side mid fielder could make along the sidelines in order to dump the ball on his own side defender. In Fig. 4.38 you can see the position of the team when the opponents are bringing the ball along the side: we are benefiting from our numerical superiority along the flank.

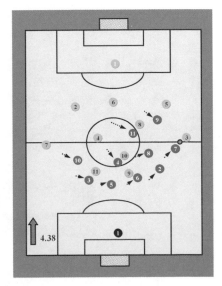

4.38

It is more difficult to manage the problem when the attacking mid fielder moves back on a central ball because, in this case, our two center mid fielders have to face no less than three opponents. In order to resolve the situation, the mid field line must keep very tight so that the two side players can give their central team mates a hand. The side backs can press the opposing center mid fielder in possession without worrying about the fact that they are leaving the other internal player without coverage. The relatively centralized position of the side mid fielder will not create problems because there is a single opponent on each flank and when our side mid fielder can't close on him, the side back can always come out to do so.

How should the defense line behave when the attacking mid fielder takes up a position near them? A defender can easily come out to mark him because the defense line is in numerical superiority against the opposing strikers (4 against 2).
When a center defender comes out to control the attacking mid fielder, the side backs must tighten in to help the center defender remaining in defense, while the side mid fielders should take (indirect) control of the opponent's side mid fielders in case they disengage themselves (Fig. 4.39).

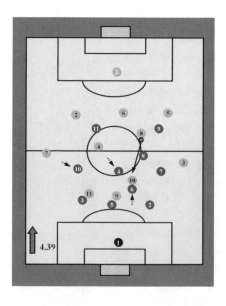

When the attacking mid fielder breaks suddenly into attack, putting our center defenders in numerical inferiority (3 against 2), the whole defense line must tighten in to make the best of our numerical advantage over the opponent's attacking players. In that way, our defenders get a 4 to 3 against their offense. Given that the defense is tightening in, in this case as well, the two side mid fielders should move back a yard or two to protect the outside corridors of the playing field.

In cases where the attacking mid fielder receives the ball near our defense line, our nearest defender must close him off while the other members of the section make a correct defensive pyramid. In shortening up on the attacking mid fielder who has just received the ball from a mid fielder, the whole back line must try to put the two opposing strikers in an offside position, making the most of the time between the moment in which the pass is made and the moment in which it is received (Fig. 4.40).

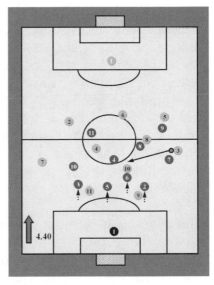

The attacking mid fielder can insert himself along the flanks without the ball, taking up position as a wing vertically placed to his own side mid fielder in possession. As you can easily imagine, the side back will have to mark him the moment he enters our defending player's zone. Should he receive the ball, our side mid fielder will immediately double team.

It is very important, in fact, to immediately double or even triple team the attacking mid fielder wherever he receives the ball. Which player should do the doubling up will depend on where the attacking mid fielder gets the ball. In the mid field he must be closed in on by a center mid fielder and a striker will double up by shifting back. If the attacking mid fielder is having difficulty (for example he is being pressed and has his back to the goal) and has no team mates who can receive the ball from him, our defense can carry out the elastic by pressing the player in possession. The two center defenders must go in to 'multiply' the marking, while the two side backs go vertically into depth. Apart from making sure there is always double diagonal coverage, the four members of the defense must be ready to move back should the attacking mid fielder manage to resolve the situation by passing to a team mate who has come to meet him and who could then

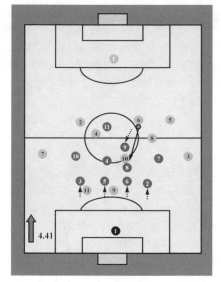

become dangerous by passing on to another player coming up from behind. Note in Fig. 4.41 how the other three mid fielders position themselves in line with the opponent in possession to prevent him from making side passes.

If the attacking mid fielder receives a central ball near the defense, he will be closed off by a center defender and doubled by the corresponding center mid fielder shifting back.
Lastly, when the attacking mid fielder receives the ball on the flank, the doubling up will be made by the pair of side players, as we have already seen.

We must make sure that the attacking mid fielder receives the ball with his back to the goal so that he cannot become a danger. To do this, we have to mark him with or without the ball, as we have already seen. Keep in mind that our opponents will be doing all they can to set up the best possible conditions for their attacking mid fielder, i.e., give him balls when he is facing our goal. To do so, the opposing mid fielders will not pass to him at once, but will give the ball first to one of the two strikers coming to meet them, and he will rebound onto the attacking mid fielder breaking in vertically. Our defense will have to be on the lookout, ready to shorten in on such a dangerous player when he is in possession, and our mid fielders must come up as soon as possible to double team.

To sum up, the attacking mid fielder must be closed off zonally, depending on his position. When he changes position, whoever was doing anticipatory marking on him must not follow but leave him to the team mate in whose direction he is going. As a result, even though he is moving around without the ball, he will not be able to create space.

Another thing we must keep in mind during the phase of non-possession is our numerical superiority along the flanks. Our pairs of side players are facing a single side mid fielder and we do not have to worry too much about the two side backs because during the offense phase they will only be giving support to the maneuvers, without moving too far into depth.

We must try to force the opponent's plays towards the sidelines by using invited pressing; and, once we have got them to this zone, we will easily be able to double up on them. Invited pressing is when you 'persuade' the opponents to pass the ball to a player who is 'convenient' to you, in this case to one of the two side mid fielders who are in numerical inferiority against our pair of side players. To do this, the team must place itself tight to invite the opposition to play out on the sidelines, where the marking can be doubled up.

This doubling up will be carried out by the side mid fielder and the side defender. If the opposing side mid fielder receives the ball near our half way line, it will be our side mid fielder to close on him while our side defender moves forward to double up; when the rival side mid fielder receives the ball near our third line our side defender will close him off while our side mid fielder moves back to double up. Doubling up on the side mid fielder can also be carried out by a side mid fielder and a striker or by a side and center mid fielder. These solutions are a lot less convenient, but they can be done whenever the side back is too far away from the part of the field in which the opposing side mid fielder receives the ball, or if he is busy in his zone marking the attacking mid fielder who has widened out onto the flank.

We must be careful with the two strikers, who will be 2 against 2 in the center. As we have already said, the side backs must tighten in so as not to leave the center defenders in a one to one (also called 'pure system') situation. The center defenders must also watch out for the strikers' 'one goes, one comes' movements to create space.

We can refer back to what was said about the 3-4-3 in connection to the pressing that the strikers will be carrying out on the three opposing defenders. They must try to steal the ball from one of the three, or force them to play towards the flanks. When one of their two side backs is in possession, one of our strikers goes to press him while the other takes up position on the passing line towards the sweeper. If the sweeper is in possession, the pair of strikers have two choices: they can either place themselves in the spaces between the sweeper and the center defenders, intervening in cases where the sweeper moves too far into depth; or they can take up axial placement. Axial placement is when one of the strikers presses the sweeper while the other places himself directly behind and in a vertical position, ready to close in on the center defender who is receiving the ball.

The side mid fielders can also close in on the two defenders widening out because against the 3-4-1-2 there are no problems of numerical inferiority on the flanks. This might, however, cause us to lose balance in the mid field, where we are in numerical equality, with the risk of finding ourselves in inferiority should the attacking mid fielder move back - and so all in all it is better if our strikers go in pressing against their side backs. Also, we prefer not to have our side mid fielders shift onto their side back in order to make the best of our numerical superiority on the flanks.

When pressing, we must reduce the distance between the players. The team must be short and compact, each single member ready to anticipate the opponent nearest to the ball.

THE 4-4-2 AGAINST THE 3-5-2

On paper, the 3-5-2 is a similar system to the 3-4-1-2. If we compare the way the two systems are placed on the field, we see one single difference: instead of the attacking mid fielder, the 3-5-2 has an extra mid fielder. In practice, however, the two systems are much different in that there is no 'creative' player in the 3-5-2, free to play along the whole attacking front.

This single difference helps us define the two teams' different styles of play.

In addition, the extra center mid fielder plays slightly behind the two other center mid fielders, who place themselves fairly wide to give him space.

For the rest, the two systems are the same: both have a three-man defense, they both have a single side player on each flank and they are both playing with a pair of strikers.

So the only important difference between the 3-5-2 and the 3-4-1-2 is their placement in the mid field.

Theoretically speaking, the 3-5-2 is a defensive system because during the non-possession phase it will usually change itself into a well-guarded 5-3-2. With the ball on the sidelines, the system often becomes a 4-4-2, with the side mid fielder on the far flank integrating himself with the defense, while his companion on the strong side remains in the mid field to press the ball. Their coach can decide to get both the side mid fielders to shift into defense even on a side ball, bringing the three center mid fielders to the flank so that one of them can press the ball.

The 3-5-2 will never carry out ultra-offensive pressing. At most they will go into pressing at around the half way line - and our defenders will be free to maneuver. The 3-5-2 will also be making very limited use of offside tactics, and their defense line plays very low around their penalty area.

Teams using the 3-5-2 very often defend man-to- man, with two side defenders marking our strikers individually and the center defender moving back to act as sweeper. It can also happen that a team lined up with this system applies a mixed zone in the defense phase, with the defenders man marking (plus the detached sweeper) and the two side mid fielders defending the flanks zonally.

This system does not give a wide range of attacking solutions during the offense phase. The fact that they only have a single player on each flank will not give them the upper hand in that part of the field, while the pair of strikers does not have the support of the attacking mid fielder and his readiness to break into play as happens with the 3-4-1-2. Also, the three defenders do not actively participate in the maneuvers but play only in support of the mid fielders.

The only strong point of the 3-5-2 is the presence of three center mid fielders, one of whom stays fixed as a point of reference for the maneuvers (the center mid fielder), while the other two (the pair of inside mid fielders) are more dynamic and so more inclined to break into play in attack and along the flanks.

As we will see, the activities of the two inside mid fielders are the only serious problem that we will face in the defense phase.

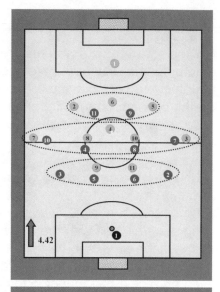

What about the numerical situation section by section? As you will see in Fig. 4.42, we are 4 against 2 in defense, in numerical inferiority; 4 against 5 in mid field; while they are in numerical superiority in attack as well (2 against 3).

We are in numerical superiority on each flank (2 against 1), there is a 2 against 2 situation at the center of the defense, they are superior in the middle of the field (3 against 2) while in attack our two strikers have to get past their three defenders.

We will now have a look at how we should behave in both phases.

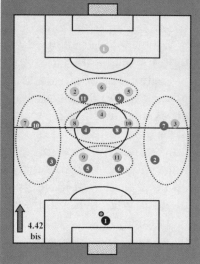

The attacking phase

Against the 3-5-2 the basic thing is to play along the sidelines during the attacking phase, where, as we have already said, our opponents are in numerical inferiority, 1 against 2. It is an even greater advantage opening play on the flanks against the 3-5-2 than against the 3-4-3 or the 3-4-1-2, because the 3-5-2 will have more difficulty resolving their numerical inferiority in this zone. Our center defenders must therefore channel play onto our two side backs to force their whole team to shift towards these players.

Having received the ball, our side back must advance until he is closed off by their side mid fielder, while our side back must sprint into depth to put their defense line under pressure. When our center mid fielders are in possession, the two side players must behave in the following way in order to create a favorable tactical situation.

With the ball in the center, and because the 3-5-2 tends to change into a 5-3-2 in the defense phase, it is a good idea for our two side mid fielders to take up a position in depth to force their two side mid fielders to remain far back. Our two side backs will now advance towards the mid field: next to our two center mid fielders there will be a lot of free space because only three of their mid fielders remain in position. In this tactical situation, the inside mid fielder in possession can choose whether to pass to the side back coming up or to the side mid fielder playing as a wing.

If we open onto the side back, they are unlikely to shift along the flanks as that would be too dangerous for them. They will probably shift the three inside mid fielders towards the flanks to close off our side back. At this point, it is easy to see that the opposite side of the field will be practically vacant, as most of their players have been drawn towards the strong side. We must make a change of play onto the weak side, where our pair of side players must be ready to carry out continuous overlapping. The two side players on the weak side must be close together, set to collaborate the moment one of the two receives the ball following a change in play (Fig. 4.43).

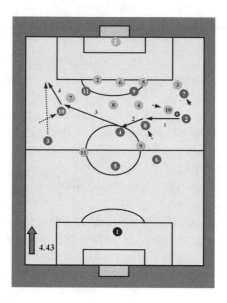

4.43

When our central mid fielder in possession passes to the side mid fielder now in position as a wing, our side back must overlap right away to put their side back 1 against 2 as he closes in. They will find it difficult to resolve this situation because the three center mid fielders are further away from the ball than in the pre-ceding case. A center defender will probably come out to mark our side mid fielder in possession, especially if their side mid fielder has moved back to cover our side defender as he is over-lapping. If the side mid fielder remains in contrast on our side mid fielder, the nearest center defender will shift out to take on our side back breaking in without the ball. Our strikers will have to try to make the most of this moment of hesitancy in our opponent's defense by going into depth, by crossing over or by cutting towards the line of the ball. Once again, if our opponents manage to neutralize our play along the flank we should make a change of play to the far side of the field.

Changes of play can, therefore, bring results even against a 3-5-2 because, as we have already shown, we will be able to make better use of our numerical superiority along the weak side of the field.
It follows that during our phase of possession we will be trying to make changes of play. To do so, we have to open play onto the flanks, keep it there for a moment in order to drag as many of

their players as possible towards us, and then quickly switch play onto the weak side of the field.

We might have trouble sending the ball horizontally from the strong to the weak side of the field if we are using the line of mid fielders alone. When the two lateral players are in depth, the remaining mid fielders are in numerical inferiority 4 to 5 against the opponent's corresponding section. And then, even if their mid fielders have shifted back alongside the defense, our two center mid fielders are still in constant numerical inferiority 2 to 3 against the others.
It follows that our changes of play must be carried out with the collaboration of the strikers and the defenders. The strikers must take turns supporting the mid fielder in possession. The defenders, on the other hand, must place themselves so that they are acting as secure relief on which to dump the ball in case of difficulty. When talking about changes of play: the strikers first of all, acting as walls for dump and rebound passes, then the mid fielders, who permit the team to effect horizontal passes that have more chance of being successful and, lastly, the defenders, receiving dumps (or maintenance passes) - all players must place themselves constantly in the 'light zone' with respect to the player in possession. You are in the 'light zone' when you are respecting the 'connection principle', i.e., when you place yourself in such a way that the player in possession can pass you the ball without there being opponents along its line who could intercept it on purpose or by accident.

It is particularly important that the whole team should help the two center mid fielders who are in numerical inferiority to the opponent's three players in this zone. Play should not be channeled onto the center mid fielders, but must pass quickly through them. During the defense phase, our opponents will try to put our center mid fielders under pressure, making the best of their numerical superiority. We must not let them do so, but as I have already said, we will have to carry out actions along the sidelines.

If one of our two mid fielders finds himself in difficulty, the two side mid fielders must modify their play, and go to meet and assist their team mate in possession, consolidating the middle line. The other center mid fielder must place himself so that his team mate can pass to him. At the same time, the nearest striker comes to meet the player in possession while the other goes into depth cutting behind his team mate (Fig. 4.44).

Against the 3-5-2 it is also important to make the best of your opponent's weak three man defense, and to do this you can use the same moves we have already seen when looking at the 3-4-3 and the 3-4-1-2. Our strik-

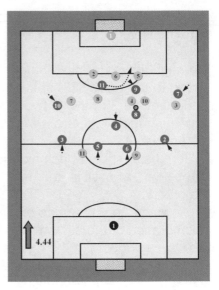

ers deviate to make the three central defenders widen out, so creating large gaps between them that can be attacked by the mid fielders breaking in. Also, as we have seen when speaking about other three-man defense systems, our strikers must make dump and rebound passes on each other to get past the defense by using speed, cutting their sweeper and center defender out of play.

The characteristic presence of the defensive rhombus in the 3-5-2 can put our pair of strikers in some difficulty. This rhombus is

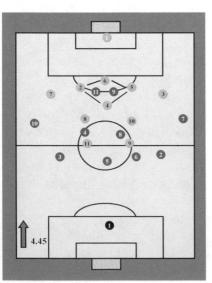

formed by the two center defenders, the sweeper and the center mid fielder playing far back in the defense phase and placing himself in the neutral zone between the defense and the mid field (Fig. 4.45).

The presence of the center mid fielder shielding the defense will create problems for our strikers, who will not easily be able to go and meet the mid fielders.

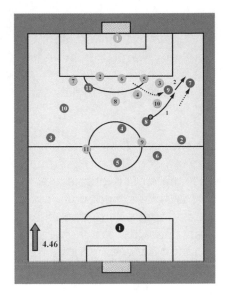

Our strikers must always play wide so as not to be caged in by the opponent's defense quartet, which effectively puts them in a situation of numerical inferiority (2 against 4). They will find space to be used at the sides of the three man defense, and when a striker receives the ball on the flank and is closed off by a side defender, our side mid fielder must always overlap to put their player in numerical inferiority (Fig. 4.46).

It is even more important, therefore, to keep the strikers wide when facing a 3-5-2.

As we said in the introduction, it often happens that a team using the 3-5-2 will be defending man-to-man or with the mixed zone. When our two strikers are being covered man to man, they must keep themselves in constant movement without the ball, making counter movements to free themselves of marking.

The strikers' movements without the ball should aim to create spaces for their team mates to break into. The opposing players will follow the strikers almost everywhere, and will not worry about the fact that certain zones get uncovered. We have to take advantage of this fact.

The movements that the strikers will be carrying out most frequently are the following:

Deviating movement. The two strikers widen out towards opposite flanks. The space created in the center will be attacked preferably by the two side mid fielders.

'Diagonal' movement. (Fig. 4.47). The two strikers sprint together towards the same flank. The space created will be attacked by a side mid or center mid fielder.

Crossovers. If they are being man marked, the strikers must carry out crossovers as well. This is a movement composed of two in-depth cuts in opposite directions. Cuts like these should be made between your nearest center defender and the sweeper.

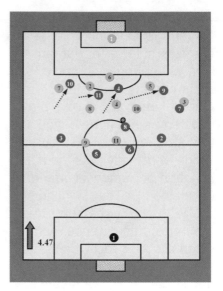

Our opponent's will hardly ever be pressing us in our own half, and so our defenders will be free to play the ball.

The finishing touch technique that we will be using most commonly is the cross from the base line. During the cross we must form an offensive triangle in the area, made up of the two strikers each placed in the zone in front of the posts and a center mid fielder breaking in to place himself behind the two strikers.

The defense phase

The first thing we must worry about in the defense phase is our numerical inferiority in the mid field, where our four players are facing five opponents.

To resolve this negative situation we need to keep our own mid field as tight as possible. The three opposing inside mid fielders must be pressed by our whole mid field line. Our two center mid fielders must close on the three rival center mid fielders and the two side players must tighten in as well to help them. Whenever they open up play towards their side players, our whole mid field line must make a diagonal onto the flank. Our side mid fielder must go to press the ball, while the entire line shifts towards the strong side, leaving the side player on the opposite flank free of marking.

Where our side mid fielder does not have time to close off his man as he receives the ball - perhaps because the player has gone too far into depth - then our side defender must come up to mark him. The whole defense line must shift position, while the side mid fielder on the opposite flank from the ball brings himself to the blind zone of the defense.

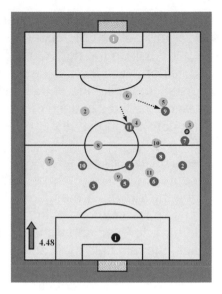

We can help the mid field section not feel their numerical inferiority by getting the strikers to move back. As well as doubling up on marking by moving back to help the center mid fielders, they can, when the ball is on the sidelines, also mark and anticipate the opponent's low lying center mid fielder (Fig. 4.48).

In fact, one of the two strikers must press the center mid fielder whenever possible.
This can happen when the striker is doubling up the marking with a team mate from the mid field, and the ball is passed from the opposing inside mid fielder in possession to the low lying center mid fielder (Fig. 4.49).

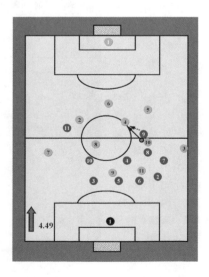

Deciding which of the two strikers must mark and anticipate the center mid fielder will depend on the position of the ball.
With the ball on the right of the field the left striker must help the mid fielders; with the ball on the left, the right striker will give assistance. While one of the strikers is doing this, the other is covering the lines in case of a possible back pass to the side defender. (c.f. Fig. 4.48).

The mid field will not always be able to get help from the strikers, because their main job is to press the three defenders.
When the strikers are engaged in pressing the defenders, and the ball passes to one of the opposing mid fielders, our own mid field have to intervene without the help of the strikers. In those cases, the mid field must act in the way we have already shown.

As we said in the introduction, the dynamism provided by its two inside mid fielders is one of the few advantages of the 3-5-2. They can:

❏   Break into depth along the sidelines when a side mid fielder is in possession on the flanks.
❏   Break into the attacking front to create problems for our defense

In the first case, our side defender must close off an inside mid fielder as he breaks in along the flanks without the ball (Fig. 4.50). This play is often used by the 3-5-2 and so our side defenders must not be taken by surprise.

In the second case, our defense must be ready to 'absorb' an inside mid fielder as he breaks into the attacking front. This is normally done as one of the two opposing strikers receives the ball after coming to meet a team mate in the mid field. When the striker receives the ball, the

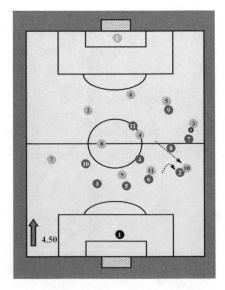

inside mid fielder overlaps on him, putting our center defender in numerical inferiority, 1 against 2, as he comes out to close on the striker.

If the defense is well-placed, the other center defender can take on the inner mid fielder breaking into the lines without the ball.

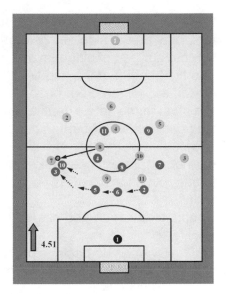

Our first center defender contin- ues to mark the striker and the two side backs tighten up to make sure that the two center players do not have to take on what are now the three attacking players (the two strikers plus the mid fielder breaking in) all by themselves.

If the defense is in difficulty, the center defender who went out to close on the striker must move back to take control of the mid fielder breaking in. The other three defenders must get compact at once, and one of them must go out straight away to contrast the striker in possession, who has been left momentarily free of marking.

Sometimes the inside mid fielder breaks into the attack before the ball has arrived to the striker, and, also here, the defense has to absorb this movement, tightening in to maintain a favorable 4 v 3.

The defense line must be careful not to concede numerical equality, which the strikers will try to exploit against our center defenders. To put a stop to this difficult situation at the center of the defense, the whole back line must keep tight, the two side backs ready to give diagonal coverage to the center defenders.

Also against the 3-5-2 we must try to channel our opponent's play along the sidelines where we are in numerical superiority 2 to 1. There is no need to worry about the presence of the two side backs, who, as we have already said in the introduction, will only be playing in support of the mid fielders.

We must apply invited pressing to induce our opponents to direct their play on the side mid fielders, who are in numerical inferiority against our pair of side players.

The tight set up of the mid field line, which we have already looked at, will force our opponents to do this.

We must immediately double team when the ball arrives to their side mid fielders. We must double team as the pass is being carried out, while the rest of the team must try to mark and anticipate other players near the action, which will make our double teaming even more effective.

Double teaming can be carried out:

❑   By our side back helped by our side mid fielder, when the opposing side mid fielder receives the ball near our penalty area.

❑   By our side mid fielder closing in and our side back moving up to help him when the opposing side mid fielder receives the ball near our mid field line. Taking away a member of the defense is not a problem because we will still be in numerical superiority in this zone. In Fig. 4.51, note how the other three players in the defense line shift their position to cover the side back who has moved forward to double up.

❑   By the side mid fielder closing in and the nearest striker moving back when the opposing side back receives the ball near his own defense line (Fig. 4.52)

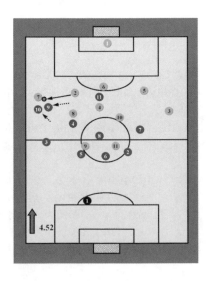

4.52

It is not a good idea for a center mid fielder to double up because, given our numerical inferiority in the mid field, we would risk compromising the situation in this zone for no good reason.

The strikers must press the three opposing defenders in the same way that we have already seen with other three man defense systems. Against a 3-5-2, if they cannot steal the ball, they must try to open up play onto the flanks, where our side mid fielder and the nearest striker will double up on the opposing side back (cf. Fig. 4.52).

In addition, the ultra-offensive pressing carried out by the two strikers on the opposing defenders will force the two side mid fielders to move back in support of their team mates. At this point, they will not be a threat in the offense phase, taking away from their team one of its few chances of creating problems for us along the flanks.

CONCLUSION

We hope that this contribution can be used as a means of discussion and confrontation. We are satisfied with the job that we have done, even if we know (and this is something we realized as we were re-elaborating the various drafts, when, again and again, some new concept was introduced or an exercise was made even clearer) that our work could be further touched up and improved and made even more interesting - though that is true of almost anything anyone ever does.
I wish to underline one thing alone: the great passion and dedication with which all the members of the group have worked to transform what was an idea into what is now a book.